Journeys
Devotions for Travelers

Journeys
Devotions for Travelers

Keith Clouten

W. WinePressPublishing
Great Books, Defined.

WinePress Publishing (PO Box 428, Enumclaw, WA 98022) functions only as book publisher. As such, the ultimate design, content, editorial accuracy, and views expressed or implied in this work are those of the author.

ISBN 13: 978-1-4141-1794-2
ISBN 10: 1-4141-1794-9
Library of Congress Catalog Card Number: 2010905027

This book is dedicated to all who journey to faraway places to perform humanitarian work for people in poverty and distress.

Contents

Preface

I AM EXCITED about journeys. I think I was born to travel. When I was just a kid in short pants, several of us boys organized our very own "Bush Rovers Club" to explore the nearby Australian countryside. Soon we upgraded to a bicycle club. Then we became excited about exploring caves that were further afield. Later, with my wife, Ngaire, and two young children, I travelled to America for further study, and then we drove around the world in a VW Camper, visiting 30 countries on the long way home to Australia. A backpacking trek of 560 miles around the Hunter Valley of eastern Australia was another unique experience. As a university library director, I travelled to five continents as a consultant, and during annual vacations, Ngaire and I organized dozens of world tours for Christian travelers. My life has been filled with journeys.

The Bible is a book about journeys. The men and women of the Bible are always on the move. Noah makes the first-ever boat trip; Abraham's travels take him all over the ancient Near East; Joseph is taken to Egypt with a caravan of traders; the Children of Israel spend 40 years on a journey to their Promised Land, and, years later, their descendants endure a forced march across the desert to the kingdom of Babylon. In New Testament times, Mary and Joseph journey from Nazareth to Bethlehem for the birth of Jesus; the wise men cross the desert to find and worship the Messiah; an Ethiopian travels to Jerusalem for the Passover and carries the gospel home to Africa; and Paul the apostle takes Christ to the world during four missionary journeys. The life of Jesus is also one of journeys; all the way from His incomprehensible journey through light years to this lost planet to the horrific journey from Gethsemane to Golgotha just to rescue us from sin and eternal death.

This little book is about the journeys undertaken by men and women of the Bible, but it also relates to the personal life journeys that each of us take along the spiritual pathway with Jesus. It is my hope that these stories will enrich your earthly journeys and my prayer that they will encourage you on your journey with Jesus.

—Keith Clouten

How to Use This Book

*Y*OU MAY USE this book of 52 devotional readings in a variety of ways. You may select one reading for each week of the year or dip into the book on successive days when you are travelling. The book is small enough to be carried in a handbag rather than in a suitcase.

Most of the readings are accompanied by a map that shows the location of the journey being discussed, supplemented with brief background notes for a better understanding of the places and the historical setting. The "Read More" segments suggest Scripture passages that tell the complete story or supplement it. If you have one of the contemporary English versions of the Bible, reading that version may help the Bible passages come alive for you. Use these additional features to extend the devotional reading two or more days of the week, or on consecutive travel days, or in any other way that you wish.

Bible Versions Used

The following Bible versions have been used in the text, with these abbreviations:

CEV   *The Holy Bible: Contemporary English Version.* Copyright © American Bible Society, 1995.

THE MESSAGE   Copyright © by Eugene H. Peterson, 1993, 1994, 1995. Used by permission of NavPress Publishing Group.

NEB   *The New English Bible.* © The Delegates of Oxford University Press and The Syndics of the Cambridge University Press 1961, 1970, 1989. Reprinted by permission.

NIV   The *Holy Bible, New International Version®, NIV®.* Copyright © 1973, 1978, 1984 by Biblica, Inc.™ Used by permission of Zondervan. All rights reserved worldwide. WWW. ZONDERVAN.COM

NKJV   The *New King James Version.* Copyright © 1979, 1980, 1982 by Thomas Nelson, Inc. Used by permission. All rights reserved.

NRSV   The *New Revised Standard Version Bible,* copyright 1989, by the

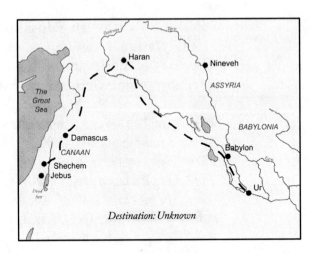

Destination: Unknown

Learn More

Abraham's family home was originally at "Ur of the Chaldees" (see Gen. 11:28). This ancient city covered four square miles. Its most prominent feature was a great stepped pyramid, or ziggurat, built to a height of 70 feet.

Abraham's long journey from Mesopotamia to Canaan occurred in two stages. First, Abraham's father, Terah, moved his entire family from Ur to Haran, located about 600 miles to the northwest (see Gen. 11:26-32). Then, at Haran, God appeared to Abraham and instructed him to leave his father's house and journey southward to Canaan (see Gen. 12:1-5).

When Abraham arrived in Canaan, his first stopping place was Shechem (see Gen. 12:6-7), located in a valley between two mountains, Gerizim and Ebal. Abraham built an altar there.

Read More

The story of how God led Abraham is told in Genesis 12:1-10. Marvel at the faith of Abraham as you read Hebrews 11:8-19. God still calls people—even families—to travel to distant lands and adapt to strange cultures to work for Him.

Destination: Unknown

*By faith Abraham, when called to go to a place
he would later receive as his inheritance, obeyed
and went, even though he did not know where he
was going....He was looking forward to the city
with foundations, whose architect and builder
is God.*

—Hebrews 11:8,10 (NIV)

"WHERE ARE WE going?" is a frequently asked
question. A mystery bus tour, lasting one
day, is usually enough to satisfy our curiosity and
our quest for adventure. We want to know where
we are going.

Think about Abraham. At mid-life, he set
out from his generational family home at Ur in
Mesopotamia with his wife, Sarah, an unreliable

nephew named Lot, a handful of servants, and all their worldly possessions on the backs of a few cantankerous camels. A Voice directed him westward to a promised land which just then was in the grip of a severe drought and looked about as promising as a desert acreage. There was no point in stopping there, so the party struggled on to Egypt, where Abraham almost lost his wife to the harem of the Pharaoh.

Returning to Canaan, Abraham and his family became semi-nomadic stock herders, a lifestyle very different from their original urban living. Then, as the sheep and cattle multiplied, a family feud erupted between Abraham and Lot's herdsmen. Deciding it would be best for them to go separate ways, Abraham gave the choice of territory to his nephew, who selfishly selected the fertile Jordan valley, leaving Abraham the rough hills. Meanwhile, the Lord's promise that He would give this country to Abraham's descendants appeared hollow, as the aging couple had no child of their own.

Most of us would have rebelled long ago, but not Abraham. He struggled on through the world, obedient to the one who directed him. And God did honor His promises to the patriarch. Isaac was born, the miracle child conceived in Sarah's old age.

Through it all, Abraham learned to trust God, though sometimes the lessons were hard. He died without seeing the "city with foundations," but he never doubted the promise. The destination might

2

be unknown, but it was never uncertain. No wonder we remember him as the Father of the Faithful.

God's plan for our lives is not always clear, but we can always trust His leadership.

Lord, teach me to trust You when I can't see the way ahead.

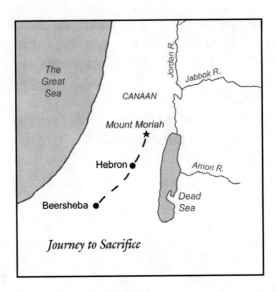

Journey to Sacrifice

Learn More

Abraham and his family settled in the region of Beersheba, a semi-arid area near the southern boundary of present-day Israel. Water was scarce there, so Abraham dug wells for his flocks and herds.

Mount Moriah, the place where Abraham travelled in obedience to God's command, is widely believed to have been the present site of the Temple Mount (also known as Dome of the Rock) in Jerusalem. The site is sacred to both Jews and Muslims. Abraham's three-day journey from Beersheba to Mount Moriah would have exceeded 50 miles.

Read More

The account of Abraham's journey to Mount Moriah is told in Genesis 22:1-19. There is much to think about in this story. Was this a case of "blind obedience" on Abraham's part, or had he learned from past experience that he could trust God completely? Have we likewise learned to "trust and obey"?

2

Journey to Sacrifice

Some years later God decided to test Abraham....
The Lord said, "Go get Isaac, your only son, the one
you dearly love! Take him to the land of Moriah,
and I will show you a mountain where you must
sacrifice him on the fires of an altar."
—Genesis 22:1-2 (CEV)

$\mathcal{T}$HE GODS OF the ancient world were demanding and to be feared. People rated a god's power and authority by the demands that he, she, or it made on them and their family. The most feared and revered gods were those who required human sacrifice—especially the sacrifice of one's own children.

Abraham lived in a multi-god society. His God was Jahweh, the one who had called him out of a pagan civilization and directed him to a land of promise. Abraham's God made some requirements of him, but the relationship took the form of a covenant, or agreement, with various obligations and privileges associated with it. Unlike other deities of his time, Abraham's God did not demand human sacrifice . . . or so it seemed, until one particular day.

Imagine the thoughts that must have raced through Abraham's mind the night God commanded him to take his only son, Isaac, on a journey to Mount Moriah and there offer him as a sacrifice. Was Jahweh really no different from the other feared gods of the ancient world? Was Jahweh about to demonstrate the same naked power and authority?

It took Abraham three days to reach Mount Moriah, every step of the journey slow and painful. At last, the altar was erected, the wood gathered, the sacrifice prepared, the last goodbyes said, and the knife raised in a trembling hand. But at that fateful moment God shouted "Stop!" Did Abraham detect a sob in God's voice as He drew the patriarch's attention to a lamb caught in the thicket?

On that journey to the mountain, God discovered something about Abraham: his unflinching loyalty and faithfulness. But perhaps even more important, Abraham discovered something about God. He learned that the heart of God's character is love—compassionate love to the utmost. This God would Himself one day become the sacrifice, dying on Calvary for your sins and mine.

It is beyond my comprehension, Lord. You gave Your life for me.

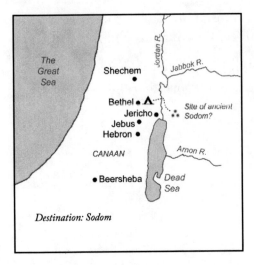

The Great Sea

Shechem

Jordan R.

Jabbok R.

Bethel ▲
Jericho
Jebus
Hebron

Site of ancient Sodom?

CANAAN

Arnon R.

Beersheba

Dead Sea

Destination: Sodom

Learn More

The location of Sodom is uncertain. Some evidence points to a site near the southern end of the Dead Sea. Recent excavations east of the Jordan River have uncovered a possible site (identified as Tall el Hammam) near the northern end of the Dead Sea.

Genesis 13 places the scene where Abraham and Lot parted company near Bethel, in an area with a commanding view of the Jordan plain near the northern end of the Dead Sea. Bethel was located on an ancient road between Shechem to the north and Beersheba to the south, and it was a significant settlement even before Abraham's time. It was while Abraham and Lot were camped there that Abraham gave his nephew the choice of land.

Read More

For the account of Lot's separation from Abraham, read Genesis 13:1-13. The destruction of Sodom is told in Genesis 19. This is the tragic story of a family that turned away from God and reaped the results of their own bad choices.

3

Destination: Sodom

*When Lot looked around, he saw there was plenty
of water in the Jordan Valley....So Lot chose the
whole Jordan Valley for himself.*
                    —Genesis 13:10-11 (CEV)

*A*FTER SETTLING IN Canaan, Abraham pros-
pered under the blessing of God. His flocks and
herds expanded, as did those of his nephew Lot. It
was soon clear that he and his nephew had to part
company in order to avoid depleting the pasture. It
was time to divide the territory.

When the patriarch invited his nephew to take
his pick of the country for his own flocks and herds,
it did not take Lot long to make up his mind. As
he stood on the escarpment, he scanned the broad,
fertile valley of the Jordan River. Plenty of feed

there. No lack of water. No need to scour the hills looking for fresh pasture and no rough hills to climb, searching for lost or injured sheep. The promise of wealth and ease.

He smiled. "Uncle Abe, I guess I'll take the Jordan Valley."

Valley living was agreeable for Lot and his family, and they loved it there. They especially liked having a city close by. For Lot, this meant having a reliable market for his meat and wool. For his wife, the city provided a source of fine clothes, jewelry, and contemporary furnishings. For his daughters, it was a magnet for social life and fun.

At first Lot might have felt uncomfortable about selling their tents and buying a house in central Sodom. The city had a particularly bad reputation for violence and immorality. As Lot watched the sun setting over the rugged mountains to the west where Abraham's encampment could sometimes be seen, he had the uneasy feeling that his uncle was praying for him each evening when the family gathered for worship. But in the end, Lot's family made the decision for him and they became residents of the city.

On the tragic day when the entire city of Sodom exploded in flames, Lot and his daughters escaped with their lives. His wife died when she disobeyed the Lord by looking back at the burning city. That evening, as Lot looked toward the western hills, his face blotched with smoke and tear stains, and clutching only the torn clothes he wore, he must have wished he had approached some of his life choices differently.

Perhaps there are some journeys that we should not take.

Lord, I ask for Your guidance in my life decisions.

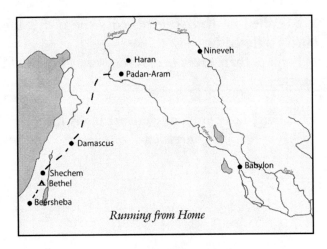

Running from Home

Learn More

Jacob's long journey to Haran began near Beersheba, where Abraham and Isaac had dug wells to provide water for their flocks and herds. Travelling north, Jacob's first stopping place was Bethel, where he slept with a rock for his pillow and was given a dream of encouragement (see Gen. 28:10-12). He apparently did not know that his grandfather Abraham had stopped at the same place soon after his arrival in Canaan and built an altar there (see Gen. 12:8-9). From Bethel, it was a long journey northward to Padan-Aram, between the Tigris and Euphrates Rivers. Jacob's uncle Laban lived in this area, close to Abraham's old family home at Haran.

Read More

Genesis 27–30 contains the complete account of Jacob's journey, beginning with the deception by which he gained the coveted birthright (see Gen. 27), the journey northward (see Gen. 28), the arrival in Haran (see Gen. 29), and his years of employment there (see Gen. 30). There is much of the local culture in this story that may limit our understanding, but there are powerful lessons about honesty and integrity that we should not miss.

4

Running from Home

Son, your brother Esau is just waiting for the time when he can kill you. Now listen carefully and do what I say. Go to the home of my brother Laban in Haran and stay with him for a while.

— Genesis 27:42-44 (CEV)

THE WORDS OF Jacob's mother keep coming back to him. Miles from home and still a long way from his uncle's place, Jacob has plenty of time to reflect on the recent upset he has caused within his family. He knows that he has messed up—but wasn't it his mother's idea for him to deceive his father, Isaac?

I only did what mother told me to do. Jacob argues bitterly with himself and with God as the memories turn over in his mind all the way to Haran.

Deception must have been imbedded in the genes of both parents. On his father's side, Grandfather Abraham once told the ruler of Egypt that Grandma Sarah was his sister, so Pharaoh claimed her for his wife. Grandfather didn't learn from that experience, because years later he said the same thing to King Abimelech. Now Jacob's mother, Rebecca, had conjured up an elaborate scheme whereby Jacob wore a hairy garment that made his blind and aging father believe that he was Esau, the firstborn. The deception worked and Jacob gained the patriarchal blessing, but Esau is now a very angry young man.

It is a long journey of 500 miles from the family home at Beersheba to Haran, but Jacob finally arrives at his uncle's farm, where he agrees to be a farm hand. Unfortunately, Uncle Laban inherited the same family genes. He promises Jacob that after seven years of service he can marry his daughter Rachel, whom the boy loves dearly. But on Jacob's wedding night Laban tricks him into sharing the bed with his older daughter, Leah. Jacob is very upset, but finally he has no option but to work another seven years to win the hand of his beloved Rachel.

Meanwhile, Jacob becomes adept at his uncle's game and finds ways to extract the best animals for his own herd. Sadly, his young sons growing up in this environment also learn from their dad. In years to come, these boys will sell their half-brother Joseph into slavery and convince their father that a wild animal has killed his favorite son.

Paul said it well: "A man reaps what he sows" (Gal. 6:7).

Lord, please help me to maintain personal integrity in everything I do and say.

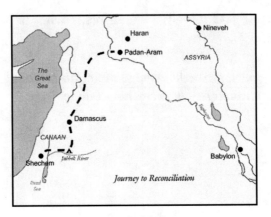

Journey to Reconciliation

Learn More

Jacob travelled south with his large family and herds and reached the River Jabbok (see Gen. 32:22). Now known as the Zarqa River, this stream meets the Jordan about midway between Galilee and the Dead Sea. Jacob's camp was probably on the route of the ancient King's Highway, a trade route from Damascus that crossed the Jabbok and continued southward along the plateau east of the Dead Sea.

After crossing the Jordan, Jacob's journey ended at Shechem, where he purchased land from the local chief and dug a well to support his livestock. Shechem was a significant place for Jacob because his grandfather, Abraham, had built an altar and worshiped there when he first arrived in Canaan (see Gen. 12:6-7).

Read More

Uncle Laban was unwilling for Jacob to leave the farm, so Jacob fled with his wives, family, and herds. Read how Laban caught up with them in Genesis 31 and the agreement they made. Genesis 32–33 tells about Jacob's camp at the Jabbok River and his meeting with Esau. Anger and bitterness still divide families. It sometimes takes just one member with a spirit of forgiveness to initiate healing.

5

Journey to Reconciliation

Jacob raised his eyes and saw Esau coming towards him with four hundred men; so he divided the children between Leah, Rachel and the two slave-girls....He then went on ahead of them, bowing low to the ground seven times as he approached his brother.

—Genesis 33:1-3 (NEB)

$\mathcal{G}$UILT-RIDDEN AND WITH a deep, gut-level fear of his brother, Jacob sets up camp on the bank of the Jabbok River. Miles still separate him from his ancestral home in Canaan. Long years span the time since the journey of his youth when he had crossed the Jordan, running scared, a lone figure with nothing but a staff and an ill-gotten birthright. Now a man of wealth, he leads a large contingent of people and animals. Within the encampment are two wives, 13 children, male and female servants, and extensive herds. He is homeward bound.

Homeward bound? Is there really any place he can call home? His family has always been nomadic tent dwellers like himself, moving flocks in search of pasture. Somewhere in Canaan he might find the graves of his parents, but nothing more. Esau lives far away in the mountains of Edom.

Thinking about Esau arouses a gnawing fear that agitates his mind like a festering sore that refuses to heal. At this very moment, according to a passing traveler, his brother is coming to meet him with 400 men. Esau must still be angry about the lost birthright and the stolen patriarchal blessing.

At nightfall Jacob falls asleep, but it is a fitful slumber. Suddenly, he is wrestling with a man on top of him. Is this Esau? Jacob, the adrenaline surging through his body, fights in a life-and-death struggle that ends with a painful dislocation of his hip. Crying out in pain—but with a death grip on the angel assailant—Jacob pleads for a blessing before releasing his hold.

The next morning, Jacob, limping with pain and trembling with uncertainty, goes ahead to meet his brother. He bows as Esau approaches, and what follows is entirely unanticipated. Esau breaks ranks with his men and runs to his brother, embracing him and kissing him. Both men weep in each other's arms, their tears of joy ending forever the long years of silence and bitterness. In all of Scripture, there is no more beautiful picture of forgiveness and reconciliation.

Lord, please give me a forgiving spirit.

Destination: Egypt

Learn More

Jacob and his family were nomadic herders, always moving
their flocks in search of pasture and water. When Joseph was
sent to find his brothers, the family encampment was in the
area known as Hebron, where Joseph's great-grandfather,
Abraham, was buried (see Gen. 37:14). Joseph expected to
find his brothers grazing their sheep several miles north near
Shechem, where the family owned a parcel of land and a well.
They were not there, but someone directed him northward to
Dothan, where he found them (see Gen. 37:16-17).

Read More

The amazing story of Joseph covers several chapters in Genesis,
beginning with chapter 37 and continuing from chapter 39
through 45. Think about the trauma and culture shock Joseph
experienced when he arrived in Egypt. We are not immune
from a similar type of culture shock when we spend time in
other parts of the world. Joseph's story also demonstrates how
God can take an evil event and still work out His purposes in
a person's life (see Rom. 8:28).

6

Destination: Egypt

When Joseph came to his brothers, they pulled off his fancy coat and threw him into a dry well. As Joseph's brothers sat down to eat, they looked up and saw a caravan of Ishmaelites coming from Gilead.

—Genesis 37:23-25 (CEV)

*I*T'S EASY TO be disliked by 10 older half-brothers when you are the favorite child of your father's favorite wife. This boy is intelligent, a born leader. Has a compulsion to organize everyone in sight. Is idolized by his sister and little brother. But he never stops talking. "Hey, listen, everyone! I had this dream where your sheaves of grain bowed down in front of mine. What can it mean?"

"Get lost, Joseph!"

His father's gift of a gorgeous multi-colored robe was the last straw. This pampered, pompous pipsqueak had to be lowered a few notches—like about 20 feet down a well. Nine of his brothers were mad enough to leave him there, but Judah voiced the idea of selling the kid to an approaching caravan of Ishmaelites. Soon, Joseph, minus his coat and his dignity, was on a slow, sad journey to Egypt.

Once the traders had made their money on the deal, the heartbroken Joseph found himself a slave at the bottom of the Egyptian social heap. After a false accusation by his master's wife, he ended up in prison. Joseph lost everything except his faith in God and a unique capacity to rise above his circumstances. Soon, with God's blessing and his natural abilities turned in the right direction, Joseph emerged from the dungeon to accept position number two in the government of Egypt. His successful strategy in protecting the country from the effects of seven years of famine made him a popular leader. He might have even made it to position number one in Egypt if he'd had a different complexion and the right accent.

Joseph's real test came when a party of sheep-herders from famine-ravaged Canaan arrived in Egypt to buy grain from his stockpile. He recognized his brothers immediately. For Joseph, it was an opportunity to exact revenge and order punishment. It was a personal struggle, but he demonstrated the compassion and forgiveness of God. He chose the healing act of reconciliation, which drew the family together in a closeness it had never known before.

Joseph's behavior toward his brothers prefigures the compassionate, forgiving love of Jesus, our own "elder brother." We need the same forgiving spirit when others hurt us.

It's hard sometimes, Lord, but I pray to forgive others as You have forgiven me.

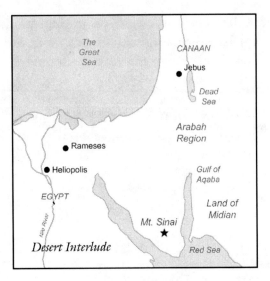

The Great Sea

CANAAN

Jebus

Dead Sea

Arabah Region

Rameses

Heliopolis

Gulf of Aqaba

EGYPT

Land of Midian

Mt. Sinai
★

Desert Interlude

Red Sea

Learn More

There is uncertainty about the exact location of the ancient land of Midian, but it may have been in northwestern Arabia, immediately east of the Gulf of Aqaba (the eastern branch of the Red Sea). Some believe that the Midianites were descendants of Abraham, because after the death of Sarah, Abraham married Keturah, and one of the six sons born to them was named Midian (see Gen. 25:1-4). The Midianites were a nomadic people, and it is possible that in the time of Moses they also occupied the lower part of the Sinai Peninsula. The burning bush experience occurred in the vicinity of Mount Horeb, which is another name for Mount Sinai.

Read More

Read the contrasting accounts of Moses the assertive young officer from Pharaoh's court in Exodus 2:11-15 and the unconfident sheepherder in Exodus 3:1-12. God chooses all kinds of people to do his work; we just need to be His willing servants.

7

Desert Interlude

Moses was minding the flock of his father-in-law,
Jethro, priest of Midian. He led the flock along the side
of the wilderness and came to Horeb, the mountain of
God. There the angel of the Lord appeared to him in
the flame of a burning bush.
—Exodus 3:1-2 (NEB)

*A*S A YOUNG man, Moses had opportunities
that were unique. No other Hebrew slave-
child got to live in an Egyptian palace. This gave
Moses superb preparation for leadership and
diplomacy.

But Moses was also an angry young man.
Court life notwithstanding, his heart bled for his
Hebrew people, who were slaves in the land. From
his advantaged position, Moses most likely used
the Egyptian archives to research the history of

his people and how and why they came to be in Egypt. One day he would write their history. One day he would become their liberator, their leader. One day!

Then it happened. He chanced upon an Egyptian officer flogging a Hebrew worker. In a moment of boiling anger, Moses intervened and killed the officer. Then, realizing what he had done, he fled for his life.

His destination was the eastern desert in the land of Midian. It was a harsh place occupied by nomadic shepherds, where survival depended on a man's ingenuity and physique. In spite of his soft palace upbringing, Moses adapted remarkably well to a nomadic existence. He was accepted into a Midianite family, married one of their daughters, and became a sheepherder, trekking the barren wastes in search of water and pasture as he mastered the techniques of wilderness survival. Gone was the ambition of liberating his people.

As the seasons rolled around, Moses became a much older and wiser man. Then, one day, God confronted him with a formidable task: Rescue His enslaved people. Moses resisted. After all, he was now just a sheepherder and had lost touch with Egyptian culture. How could he address Pharaoh when he hadn't spoken Egyptian for 40 years?

But God persisted, and Moses became the leader of the Exodus. So God's plan for Israel's deliverance was not jeopardized. In fact, Moses' unique background in Egyptian diplomacy, wilderness survival, and sheep management turned out to be the very mix of skills that God needed.

Never underestimate what God can do with your abilities when you give them to Him.

Lord, I often feel like Moses did in the desert,
not gifted to do very much. All the same,
make me a willing servant.

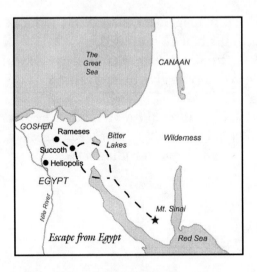

Escape from Egypt

Learn More

Which way did they go? There are various theories about the route the Israelites took on the Exodus and the identity of Mount Sinai. Was Mount Sinai one of the peaks on the eastern side of the Gulf of Aqaba? Or was it the traditional mountain near the southern end of the Sinai Peninsula? There is also uncertainty about the identity of the biblical "Red Sea," or, literally, "Sea of Reeds." Did the miraculous crossing of the water take place on the Gulf of Suez, or did it take place at one of the "Bitter Lakes" north of the Gulf? These shallow lakes were largely absorbed with the construction of the Suez Canal. We may never know the answer to these questions.

Read More

Exodus 13:17–14:31 records the story of the departure of the Israelites from Egypt and the miraculous crossing of the sea. Throughout the journey, the Israelites had a great deal to learn about trusting God in all circumstances. We need to learn that lesson on our life journey as well.

8

Escape from Egypt

*When Pharaoh let the people go, God did not lead them
on the road through the Philistine country, though
that was shorter. For God said, "If they face war, they
might change their minds and return to Egypt." So
God led the people around by the desert road toward
the Red Sea.*

—Exodus 13:17-18 (NIV)

THE DAY OF deliverance had come. The large
company of Israelites set out from the Egyptian
city of Rameses, where they had been enslaved for so
long. Avoiding the direct military road from Egypt
to Palestine, they followed a desert road eastward
in the general direction of the "Red Sea" ("Sea of
Reeds" in the original Hebrew).

Their first stop was at Succoth, and then Etham at the edge of the desert. There, the Lord did a strange thing. He instructed Moses, "Tell the Israelites to turn back and encamp near Pi Hahiroth, between Migdol and the sea." We do not know the location of those places, but it was clearly a change of direction. Why? Moses must have wondered what the Lord had in mind, so God graciously explained: "Pharaoh will think you are all wandering around the land in confusion, hemmed in by the desert. He will decide to pursue you, but don't worry. I have a plan that will bring victory to you and great glory to Myself."

The Israelites were soon camped in the wilderness with a sea in front of them and an advancing Egyptian army behind them. Terrified, they cried to Moses, "What have you done to us by bringing us out of Egypt? It would have been better for us to serve the Egyptians than to die in the desert!"

Then God unfolded His plan, which involved a miraculous crossing of the water. After the destruction of the Egyptian army, the Israelites were able to continue their journey without fear of further attack from that quarter. It was the first of many miracles and lessons that would demonstrate to a people emerging from slavery that their God was powerful and caring. If they would trust Him, listen and obey His instructions, and respect His chosen leader, Moses, they would arrive safely and soon in their Promised Land.

God is not stumped by obstacles in our paths. He sees the end from the beginning.

You know the way through the wilderness, Lord. I can trust Your leadership.

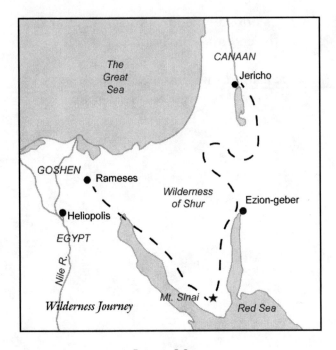

Learn More

The above map illustrates the traditionally accepted route of the Israelites down the Sinai Peninsula and then through the barren wilderness northward toward Palestine. Because of uncertainties regarding the ancient methods of counting men and families, we cannot be sure as to the actual number of Israelites who made the journey.

Read More

Read Exodus 15:22-27 and Exodus 16–17 to learn about the variety of difficulties the Israelites faced as they travelled through strange desert terrain. Read about how they had to grow accustomed to new and strange food, learn about water quality, and confront warlike tribes from the desert. They were almost totally dependent on God for their survival.

9

Wilderness Journey

The whole congregation of the Israelites complained against Moses and Aaron in the wilderness. The Israelites said to them, "If only we had died by the hand of the Lord in the Land of Egypt."
—Exodus 16:2-3 (NRSV)

WILDERNESS BACKPACKING AND sleeping in a pup-tent may be loads of fun for some, but it can be a horrible adventure for anyone unprepared for camping outdoors without the modern conveniences of home.

Consider the plight of the Israelites as they commenced their wilderness journey. For centuries they and their ancestors had been house-dwellers, day laborers or slaves, crowded into Egyptian slums. Suddenly, they had to abandon that lifestyle and become nomads in a harsh desert environment. It demanded change on a big scale. Wilderness survival required totally new skills such as tent construction, breeding and managing herds of sheep and goats, discovering new food sources from plants and wildlife, finding good and reliable water supplies, learning to recognize poisonous plants and reptiles, and dealing with marauding parties of tribal peoples. Little wonder the Israelites cried for the settled and predictable life back in Egypt. It was a miracle that they survived the desert experience at all.

The Israelites could not have survived without the strong and capable leadership of Moses, who had 40 years of experience in the desert as a shepherd. However, Moses could not handle the job alone, even with the advice of his wise father-in-law, Jethro. The Israelites survived only because God was their ultimate leader, teacher, and guide. On numerous occasions the Lord rescued these ill-prepared and faithless people through dramatic miracles. Moses was simply His appointed manager—a willing and obedient servant-leader.

God's purpose in the Exodus involved leading the Israelite community out of slavery in Egypt to nationhood in the land He had promised to Abraham long before. It took 40 years of hardship and training in the wilderness for them to develop the character, organization, and skills needed to settle Canaan and become fully God's chosen nation.

God still calls individuals to abandon the familiar and comfortable and serve Him in strange and formidable places. Survival always demands trust in the divine Leader, who still specializes in miracles.

Teach me to trust You, Lord, wherever my journeys take me.

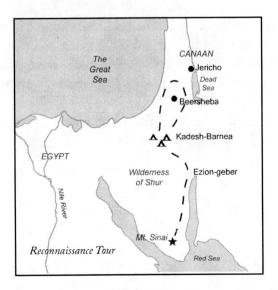

The Great Sea

CANAAN

Jericho

Dead Sea

Beersheba

Kadesh-Barnea

EGYPT

Wilderness of Shur

Ezion-geber

Nile River

Mt. Sinai

Reconnaissance Tour

Red Sea

Learn More

Israel was encamped at Kadesh-Barnea when Moses assembled 12 individuals to undertake a reconnaissance tour northward into the territories occupied by the Philistines and Canaanites (see Num. 13:1-16). The exact location of Kadesh-Barnea is not known, but there are permanent springs of water in the desert south of Beersheba. After the return of the spies, Israel travelled and camped throughout the wilderness for another 40 years before moving up the eastern side of the Dead Sea, crossing the Jordan, and beginning the conquest of Canaan at Jericho (see Josh. 5:13).

Read More

Read about the courage of Caleb and Joshua in Numbers 13:26-33 and 14:1-9. God later appointed Joshua to lead the Israelites after Moses' death (see Josh. 1:1-9). You can also read Caleb's amazing testimony in Joshua 14:6-12. God still needs individuals like Caleb and Joshua who will stand for truth and right, courageous in the face of pressure and hostility.

Reconnaissance Tour

The Lord said to Moses, Choose a leader from each tribe and send them into Canaan to explore the land I am giving you.
            —Numbers 13:1-2 (CEV)

*A*FTER YEARS OF desert living and harsh wilderness wandering, the Israelites are encamped at Kadesh-Barnea, poised for a northward advance into Canaan. But warring tribal clans occupy their Promised Land, so Moses chooses 12 men for a reconnaissance mission. It is a risky undertaking, as the men are to thoroughly explore the territory, noting patterns of settlement, water supplies, and agriculture. If possible, they will return with samples of the country's produce.

For men now accustomed to life in a barren wilderness, the territory of Canaan seems like a tropical paradise. Their eyes feast on green valleys, olive groves, manicured vineyards, date palms, and waving fields of wheat and barley. This is indeed a fertile country. As evidence, they collect as much fruit as they can carry back to their desert encampment.

The explorers are also overwhelmed by the walled cities. The strangers, used to a nomadic existence with mere tents for shelter, gawk at the stone fortifications that encircle each town. This is surely a technologically advanced society whose inhabitants are head-and-shoulders above themselves.

Returning safely to their sunburned countrymen, the expedition members give their report. All 12 agree that the fertility of the land defies description. "Just try to imagine," they say, "a land flowing with milk and honey!" The listeners shake their heads in wonder and excitement.

"But you should see the walled cities," they continue. "Vast fortifications, great cities, frightening! And the inhabitants are fearsome men of enormous size! Enough to strike terror to any heart! We were like grasshoppers alongside them!"

The people shiver in fear and cling to each other. "Let's stay here in the desert," they say. "Let's find a new leader and go back to Egypt," some say. The dream of a longed-for Promised Land has turned into a nightmare of frightening possibilities.

There is also a minority report from two expedition members, Caleb and Joshua, who present a balanced account of man's engineering pitted against the power of God Almighty. But nobody listens to them, so the Israelites are forced to wander in the wilderness for another 40 years.

Like Caleb and Joshua, Christians today are privileged to have a different view of our world.

Forgive me, Lord, for the times when I
overlook Your power and purpose.

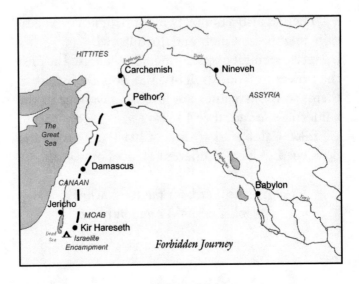

Forbidden Journey

Learn More

Pethor is mentioned twice in the Old Testament (Num. 22:5 and Deut. 23:4), with references to the Euphrates River and to Mesopotamia. There is some archaeological evidence that Pethor was the ancient Hittite city of Pitru, located about 20 miles south of Carchemish, the Hittite capital. Balaam may have been a priest-diviner and a renowned curser. His journey from Pethor to Moab must have been at least 400 miles.

The territory of the Moabites extended along a high plateau that rose abruptly from the east shore of the Dead Sea.

Read More

Numbers 22 tells the story of a prophet who valued money more than doing the will of God. His attempts to curse Israel were a failure; blessings came from his mouth instead (see Num. 23–24). Material wealth and love of money does not buy happiness or eternal life, as Jesus' parable of the rich fool in Luke 12:16-21 demonstrates.

11

Forbidden Journey

Balaam was riding his donkey to Moab, and two
of his servants were with him. But God was angry
that Balaam had gone.

—Numbers 22:22 (CEV)

W E KNOW LITTLE about Balaam; only that he
lived at a place called Pethor near the River
Euphrates and that he had some reputation as a holy
man or prophet.

Far away to the south, hordes of Israelites were
moving relentlessly northward, emerging from the
desert as they travelled toward their long-promised
land. Watching them nervously from the heights
above the Dead Sea, the Moabites feared the Israelites
would invade their territory. King Balak of Moab
was determined to do something about it, so he
dispatched messengers to Balaam.

"Please come and curse Israel," he said. "I will pay you well."

The Lord told Balaam to stay home, but the offer of a handsome reward persuaded the prophet to go. So he saddled his donkey and set out on the rather long journey to Moab.

The first sign of trouble came when the donkey turned off the road into a field. Balaam beat the animal, and they set off again. When they came to a narrow part of the road with rock walls on either side, the donkey veered to one side, crushing Balaam's foot against the rocks. Hurt and angry, the willful prophet gave another savage hiding to his beast, and they set off once more, only to have the animal lie right down underneath him. Exasperated, Balaam began a third beating of his donkey when the animal suddenly opened its mouth and said, "What have I done to you to make you beat me these three times?" Balaam was so mad and out of his tree at that moment that he answered right back: "Because you have made a fool of me!" The Lord's angel soon interrupted the conversation (after he had stopped laughing, I think) and gave some clear instructions to Balaam.

The Lord has many ways at His disposal to get a message across to someone who doesn't want to listen. He will set up barriers to get your attention as you go through the journey of life. But if you are ever addressed by your dog, donkey, or cockatoo, you'll know that God is nearing the end of his options!

> *Lord, keep me from doing stupid things that will get me into trouble.*

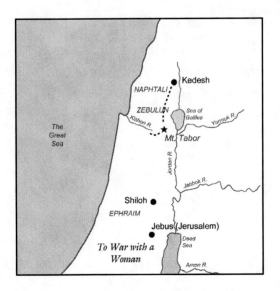

Learn More

Kedesh was one of the Canaanite strongholds conquered by Israel under the leadership of Joshua (see Josh. 12:22). Later, this region became a part of northern Palestine and was assigned by lot to the tribe of Naphtali. The city was also one of six Israelite "cities of refuge" for anyone guilty of unintentional homicide (see Josh. 20:7).

The Kishon River flows southward from the slopes of Mount Tabor and then in a northwesterly direction to reach the Mediterranean Sea near Mount Carmel. The modern name of the river is Nahr el-Mokattah, meaning "river of slaughter"— perhaps a reference to the defeat of Sisera and years later, to the slaughter of the prophets of Baal (see 1 Kings 18:40).

Read More

Try to find a contemporary English translation to make this story in Judges 4–5 come alive. In a male-dominated society and culture, God did not limit His choice for a leader.

12

To War with a Woman

Deborah and Balak left for Kedesh, where Barak called together the troops from Zebulun and Naphtali. Ten thousand soldiers gathered there, and Barak led them out from Kedesh. Deborah went too.
                              —Judges 4:9-10 (CEV)

*I*T HAPPENED DURING the darkest days in Israel's history. Without a king or central government, there was structural chaos and moral disintegration in the land. In the words of Scripture, "Everyone did whatever seemed right in their own eyes." For 20 years a Canaanite army, led by a fearsome general named Sisera, harassed the two northern tribes of Naphtali and Zebulun.

In desperation, the people cried to God for help, and He acted quickly, revealing his plan to Deborah, a prophetess and judge who lived away to the south. Deborah immediately sent a messenger to fetch Barak, an Israelite leader who lived at Kedesh in the distressed province of Naphtali. Barak responded, and an interesting conversation ensued.

"Barak," Deborah said, "the Lord commands you to select 10,000 men from Naphtali and Zebulun and lead them to Mount Tabor. The Lord will lure Sisera there, with his chariots and troops, and will give them into your hands."

Barak balked at the assignment. He knew that 10,000 Israelites would be no match for the Canaanite army with their iron chariots. And Barak was not accustomed to taking orders from a mere woman, even if she was a judge. So he formulated his response.

"All right, if you go with me to the battle, I'll do it. But if you don't go with me, I won't go." He chuckled to himself. There was no way that a woman would join the men in a battle!

Deborah's response shocked him. "Of course I'll go with you. But understand that with an attitude like that, there will be no glory in it for you. God will use a woman's hand to take care of Sisera."

Wow! Barak felt cornered, but he faithfully did what he was asked to do. He gathered an army and went into battle, accompanied by Deborah. At the Kishon River, they met Sisera's army with 900 iron chariots. With the blessing of God, however, Sisera and his chariots were completely routed in a smashing victory, and Sisera himself finished the day with a tent peg driven through his skull—by a woman named Jael.

Never assume that God will do it your way!

Lord, You often make Your plans known through godly people. Help me to listen.

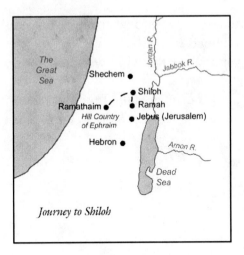

Journey to Shiloh

Learn More

Where is Ramah? Several sites in Israel have been associated with the name. In the story of Hannah and Elkanah, a village called Ramathaim is located in "the hill country of Ephraim" (1 Sam. 1:1, NIV), but this area has vague boundaries. The two places most often identified with Samuel's birthplace and later residence are shown on the map.

Shiloh was located between Bethel and Shechem (see Judg. 21:19), about 20 miles north of Jerusalem. Shiloh was the place where the Israelites set up their tent tabernacle soon after they entered Canaan. The tabernacle remained there through the period of the judges. During Samuel's time, the Philistines captured the sacred ark, and the tabernacle was destroyed soon afterward.

Read More

The first three chapters of 1 Samuel record the story of Hannah and the birth of Samuel. In a time of widespread apostasy and neglect of spiritual things, Elkanah and his family were faithful and regular in their worship attendance. Are we as faithful today in our worship?

13

Journey to Shiloh

*Elkanah lived in Ramah, a town in the hill country
of Ephraim....Elkanah had two wives, Hannah
and Peninnah. Although Peninnah had children,
Hannah did not have any.*

—1 Samuel 1:1-2 (CEV)

*P*LEASE, LORD, IF You will only understand my
misery and give me a son, then I will give him
to You for all the days of his life." It was a desperate
prayer from a troubled woman.

This story comes from the period of the judges
in Israel. The days were evil, as Israel had lapsed
into idolatry. Families were supposed to travel to
Shiloh each year to worship at the sacred tabernacle,
make sacrifices, and renew their vows of faithfulness, but most Israelites now neglected this solemn
duty. There were, however, a few good people like

Elkanah, the man of our story, who faithfully took his family to Shiloh each year to worship and make sacrifices to the Lord.

There was sadness in Elkanah's home, however, because his wife, Hannah, had borne no children. That in itself was reason enough for him to take a second wife, as a childless marriage was considered a curse and grounds for divorce. Yet Elkanah loved Hannah more than his other wife, which caused jealousy and unpleasantness in the home. Hannah was often in tears. It was during one of the annual visits to Shiloh that she poured out her heart to God, pleading for a son.

God responded to Hannah's prayer, and a baby boy was born to her. She named him Samuel and kept her promise by dedicating him to God's service when he was four years old. It was hard for Hannah to kiss her little son goodbye and leave him in the care of the high priest, Eli, in Shiloh, but she had prepared herself and little Samuel for this day. She would not forget him. Each year she returned and presented her growing boy with a robe made especially for him.

God had something special in mind for Samuel. While he was still a child, he was awakened one night by the voice of God and given an important message for Eli and all Israel. It marked the beginning of a prophetic ministry that opened a new chapter in Israel's history. Before he died, Samuel dedicated another boy, David, as the future king of Israel.

Even in the darkest times of history, God has found faithful men and women willing to carry forward His work.

I want to be Your faithful follower, Lord, always listening for Your voice.

To Moab and Back

Learn More

The land occupied by the Moabites was a high plateau intersected by deep valleys located east of the Dead Sea. In the time of Naomi and Ruth, the northern boundary of Moab was approximately the Arnon River. One of the greatest trade routes of the ancient world—the King's Highway from Damascus to Egypt—passed though Moab. The Moabites worshipped their god, Chemosh.

Bethlehem, best known as being the birthplace of Jesus (see Luke 2:1-7), was located six miles south of Jerusalem. Years before, it was also the birthplace of David, the youngest son of Jesse and great-grandson of Ruth and Boaz.

Read More

The book of Ruth is an inspiring section of the Old Testament. Its four chapters contain the entire account of Naomi and Ruth. How does the story of Ruth help us to be more understanding of people from other cultures?

14

To Moab and Back

So Naomi returned from Moab accompanied by
Ruth the Moabitess, her daughter-in-law, arriving in
Bethlehem as the barley harvest was beginning.
                                    —Ruth 1:22 (NIV)

ELIMELECH AND NAOMI live with their two boys in the rural town of Bethlehem when a severe drought grips the land. With hunger staring them in the face, Elimelech decides to take his young family someplace else. Packing their goods on a couple of donkeys, they bid farewell to their neighbors and friends, cross the Jordan River, and journey eastward up the steep hills to Moab. This is an unfriendly foreign country, but for now it offers respite from the famine.

The years roll by, and the boys grow to manhood and marry Moabite women. Then death strikes the family three times. First Elimelech dies, and then the two sons, leaving three widows behind: mother Naomi and two childless daughters-in-law, Orpah and Ruth.

Without their protective breadwinners, life becomes a case of survival for the women. So Naomi decides to pack what little she has and return to Bethlehem, where times of plenty have replaced the years of famine. She wants to go alone, but the two younger women beg to accompany her. Naomi tries to dissuade them, telling them that they are Moabites, with a religion and culture of their own. She knows how hard it is to migrate to a foreign country. Orpah is finally convinced, but Ruth insists on making the journey with her mother-in-law. "Your people will be my people," she says, "and your God will be my God."

Their arrival in Bethlehem at the time of the barley harvest creates a stir in the town. *Who is this old woman, her face battle-lined beyond her years? Is this really Naomi? Where is Elimelech, and the two boys? And who is the strange young woman with her?* Naomi tells her sad story.

Yet the story has a happy ending. Ruth made a successful adjustment to the customs and culture of Israel. She met and married Boaz, a kind and generous man from the same clan as Elimelech. The birth of their son, Obed, brought joy to Ruth and to the aging Naomi. Ultimately, Obed became the grandfather of the great King David, and it was through that royal line that Jesus was born.

God sometimes leads us through dark and lonely paths, but He gives grace and strength for the journey.

*Lord, I pray for compassion and understanding
when I encounter displaced people.*

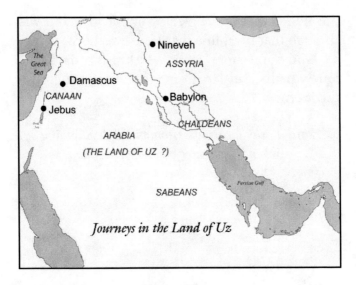

Journeys in the Land of Uz

Learn More

The Land of Uz was probably somewhere in Arabia. Job is identified as "the greatest of all the people of the East" (Job 1:3), which would place his home somewhere east of Palestine. Job 1:15-17 tells how the Sabeans (who probably came from southern Arabia) and the Chaldeans (who came from what is now southern Iraq) attacked his farm.

Some scholars believe that Job belongs to the time of the patriarchs, as the picture of life described in the book of Job fits the time period of Abraham, Isaac, and Jacob (approximately 1800 B.C.).

Read More

You can capture highlights of Job's story by reading these selections: Job 1–2; 3:1-13; 16:1-5; 38:1-41; 42:1-6. Also be sure to read how Job was blessed in his later years in Job 42:10-17. If only we could see the end from the beginning—but that's exactly why we must learn to trust our Father.

Journeys in the Land of Uz

When Job's three friends...heard about all the troubles that had come upon him, they set out from their homes and met together by agreement to go and sympathize with him and comfort him.

—Job 2:11 (NIV)

THE STORY COMES from long ago and far away. Job is introduced as one of the wealthiest men of his time—a rancher with a large family, thriving flocks of sheep, camels, oxen, and donkeys, and lots of servants to care for everything. Then calamity strikes, and within a short time Job loses everything he owns, including his family and his health. The man has nothing left except a nagging wife and an unshakeable faith in God.

When the news reaches the world outside, three of his friends decide to go visit him. Together they arrive at Job's farm, or what remains of it. As they approach Job, they are in shock, hardly recognizing their old friend as he sits in the ruins of his house, covered with painful sores.

We think of the three visitors as "Job's comforters," and, in fact, they did some of the things that comforters should do. They wept with him and then sat in respectful silence for a long time, waiting for Job to express his emotions.

When it came, it was a long outburst of sorrow. "Curse the day when I was conceived," he cried. "Why didn't I die as soon as I was born? I have no peace, no rest, only turmoil."

When Job was done, his friends responded. They tried—less wisely now—to give him advice, even suggesting that he might have brought the calamity on himself. "Blessed is the man whom God corrects," Eliphaz intoned, perhaps quoting an ancient Scripture. "You should not despise the discipline of the Almighty."

At the end of the visit, Job himself gave the would-be comforters some sound advice. "To him who is afflicted, kindness should be shown by his friend," he admonished. "You are miserable comforters! If I were in your place, it would be easy to criticize or to give advice." Then he added, "But I would offer hope and comfort instead."

Before the three left, Job prayed for them. I like to think that they returned home a bit kinder and wiser.

Lord, teach me to be kind and wise, especially in circumstances of bereavement or loss.

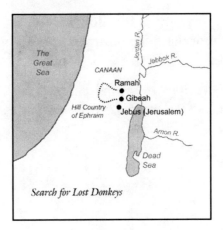

Search for Lost Donkeys

Learn More

Saul's family home was at Gibeah, a short distance north of Jerusalem. After becoming king, he established his fortress and royal residence there.

There is uncertainty about the location of Ramah, the home of Samuel. As one of the judges of ancient Israel, he conducted a circuit of four towns in the territory of Benjamin, where he held court to settle disputes.

Much of the tribal territory of Ephraim was hill country. The "hill country of Ephraim" was probably part of what is now known as the Shephelah, a region of rolling hills and shallow valleys west of Jerusalem.

Read More

Read 1 Samuel 9:1-27 and 10:1-19 for the details of this story. During Samuel's time, the Israelites began clamoring for a king to rule over them. God foresaw the consequence of their choice, but He did not force His will upon them (see 1 Sam. 8:4-22). In the same way, sometimes we make bad decisions. We may have to live with the consequences, but God does not abandon us.

16

Search for Lost Donkeys

Now the donkeys of Kish, Saul's father, had strayed.
So Kish said to his son Saul, "Take one of the boys
with you; go and look for the donkeys."
—1 Samuel 9:3 (NRSV)

EXCUSE ME, SIR. Have you seen any stray donkeys?"

Farmer Kish, who lived in the town of Gibeah, had lost some donkeys and had decided to send his son, Saul, to find them. This lad was unusually tall and lanky, head-and-shoulders above other kids of the same age. He was also mature for his years, which was why his father had given him the task of finding the lost animals. Saul was not to go alone, though—a trusted servant would accompany him. The two set out together, searching through the hill country of Ephraim, northwest from Gibeah.

"Have you seen any stray donkeys around here?"

It seemed to be a lost cause. Finally, after three days of searching through the hills, the two found themselves in the district of Zuph. Frowning, Saul spoke up. "I think we'd better go back, or my father will stop thinking about the donkeys and start worrying about us." The servant understood, but had a suggestion. "Look, in the town of Ramah near here lives a man of God, a seer. Perhaps he can tell us where the donkeys are."

As the two headed toward the town gate, they met some young ladies coming out to draw water from the village well. Saul's companion asked the whereabouts of the seer, and they were soon directed to the prophet Samuel who, it turned out, was expecting them. "Don't worry about the donkeys," the prophet said to the concerned young Saul, "they have been found. But God has a very special assignment for you."

Samuel produced a flask of oil and anointed the lad who was to become the king of Israel. An assignment indeed! Saul, taken completely by surprise, reminded the prophet that he was just a kid from a small family, belonging to the smallest of the 12 tribes of Israel. It didn't matter. God knew who He was looking for.

Sometimes God amazes us. Don't be surprised if even a journey to find some stray animals turns into something much bigger.

Lord, wherever my journeys take me, please keep me open to Your leading. Help me to accept whatever You have in mind for my life.

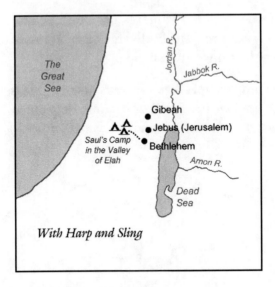

With Harp and Sling

Learn More

David's family home was in Bethlehem. As a youth, he travelled often to King Saul's fortress at Gibeah, where he played his harp for the king. His boyhood trip to the battlefront where he confronted Goliath took him to the Valley of Elah, northwest of Jerusalem. Elah was located in what is known as the Shephelah, a region of shallow valleys that lie in a generally east-west direction inland from the coastal plain. Several battles were waged in these valleys between the Philistines and the men of Israel. On this occasion, the Philistines were camped on one side of the Elah valley, while the men of Israel faced them on the opposite slopes.

Read More

First Samuel 17 tells the story of David and Goliath. David's youthful audacity and success led to jealousy and anger on the part of his oldest brother, Eliab (see 1 Sam. 17:28), and King Saul (see 1 Sam. 18:6-9). Jealousy is an evil, soul-destroying vice.

17

With Harp and Sling

*One day Jesse said to David, "Take this bushel of
roasted grain and these ten loaves of bread to your
brothers. Give this cheese to their captain and see
how the boys are getting along; and bring us back
a letter from them."*
—1 Samuel 17:17-18 (TLB)

$\mathcal{I}$T WAS NOT easy being the youngest son in
a large family of boys. David, left at home to
take care of the sheep while his older siblings were
serving in King Saul's army, yearned to be with them
at the battlefront. He was a brave and capable lad,
strong as a lion, but something of an enigma to his
family. This boy combined masculine strength with
a love of music and poetry. David and his harp were
inseparable. While caring for the sheep, he would sit

and compose songs that came from his heart, words of praise to his very personal God—one who, like himself, combined the strength and gentleness of a shepherd.

The day when David set out with food for his brothers began innocently enough. Early in the morning, he loaded provisions on the donkey, said goodbye to his father, picked up a sling (in case he encountered a lion or bear along the way), and set out. How could he have guessed that before the day was over he would use that simple sling to kill a Philistine giant who had terrorized the army of Israel? It took the audacious courage of a boy with faith in an invincible God to accomplish the impossible.

For David, that short trip from Bethlehem to the valley of Elah was the commencement of a lifetime journey that led to fame and glory. But the path also led through dark and dangerous valleys. There were times of triumph and times of defeat, years of godly leadership tainted with moments of human weakness. Throughout the journey, though, there was always the legacy from his boyhood years on the farm—the courage of a lion, the heart of a shepherd, and an unquenchable faith in God.

Life has its ups and downs, but, like David, we can always keep a song in our heart.

*My life is full of peaks and valleys, Lord.
Please keep me courageous and faithful
in all circumstances.*

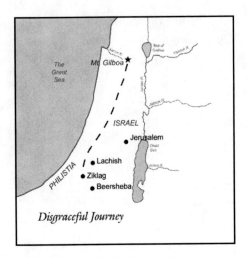

Disgraceful Journey

Learn More

Mount Gilboa, where Saul's army met the Philistines, is the highest point along a ridge of hills overlooking the Esdraelon Valley.

The town of Ziklag had been allocated to the tribe of Judah during the Israelite conquest of Canaan, but by the time of King Saul it had fallen into Philistine hands. The Philistines perceived David to be a threat to Saul, who was at war with them, which explains why the Philistine king, Achish, was willing to grant Ziklag to David.

Read More

Scripture records two slightly different versions of the death of Saul. First Samuel 31 records how Saul took his own life by falling on his sword. Second Samuel 1:1-16 recounts how David learned of Saul's death when a young Amalekite arrived and claimed that he had killed the wounded king. Was David unduly harsh with the young Amalekite? Contrast the young man's unscrupulous behavior with David's integrity and respect for God's anointed.

18

Disgraceful Journey

*On the third day after Saul's death a man came from
the army with his clothes rent and dust on his head.
When he came into David's presence he fell to the
ground in obeisance.*

—2 Samuel 1:2 (NEB)

*K*ING SAUL WAS at Mount Gilboa with his
army, battling the Philistines. He had survived
several skirmishes with the Philistines, but this
battle was to prove his nemesis. Three of his sons,
including Jonathan, David's close friend, died in the
battle. Then Saul himself was mortally wounded.
Sensing that his end was near, he cried to his
armor-bearer to run him through with his sword.
Terrified, the armor-bearer refused, so Saul took his
own sword and fell on it.

A young Amalekite witnessed the event and seized an opportunity. Quickly stripping Saul's body of his crown and armband, the man dashed away with his treasures and formulated a plan. Knowing that David, the young commander, was destined to be Israel's next king, he decided that he would be the first to break the news to him. David would surely be pleased to hear of Saul's death, and he might reward whoever was responsible. It was an exciting idea—especially if he could present David with Saul's crown and armband!

Learning that David was at Ziklag, three days' journey southward, the young man set out. There was no time to lose. Not even time to shave and clean up.

"Where have you come from?" David asked the bedraggled young fellow who fell on the ground before him. After the man told him that he had come from the battlefront, David asked, "What happened? Tell me."

So the smug young man spun his tale. "I was there, and I saw Saul was wounded and leaning on his spear," he lied. "He called out to me and said, 'Stand over me and kill me, because I am going to die anyway.' So I killed him and took the crown that was on his head and his armband and I've brought them to you, my lord."

The man paused, waiting for the praise, but his hopes quickly died. David was furious. "Why were you not afraid to lift your hand to destroy the Lord's anointed? Go, strike him down!" he commanded. And the young man's disgraceful journey ended right there in a pool of his own blood.

Lord, may I never sacrifice integrity for
ambition or personal gain.

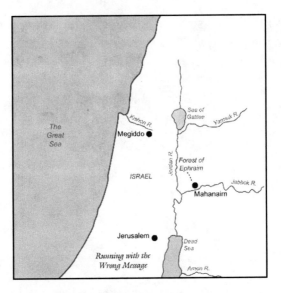

Map showing The Great Sea, Kishon R., Megiddo, Sea of Galilee, Yarmuk R., Jordan R., Forest of Ephraim, Mahanaim, Jabbok R., ISRAEL, Jerusalem, Dead Sea, Amon R.

Running with the Wrong Message

Learn More

The location of the battle was the Forest of Ephraim, which lay east of the Jordan River. The region is now arid, but in biblical times there were many areas of forest—even dense forest—in places where there is now grassland or desert.

Just to the south of the Forest of Ephraim was the town of Mahanaim, the site of a fortress alongside the Jabbok River. This is possibly near the place where Jacob camped and met Esau during his journey back to Canaan. David fled to this fortress for safety during the rebellion of Absalom and waited there while the final battle was in progress.

Read More

Read the full account of this battle between David and Absalom in 2 Samuel 18:1-33. The young priest, Ahimaaz, was himself the son of Zadok, the high priest at that time. As we learn in this story, it is usually unwise to seek a responsibility for which we are not fitted.

19

Running with the Wrong Message

Ahimaaz, Zadok's son, said, "Let me run to the king
and bring him the good news that God has delivered
him from his enemies."
—2 Samuel 18:19 (THE MESSAGE)

*I*N ANCIENT TIMES, before cell phones or the
Internet or even horseback, news had to be
carried on foot. Professional runners were employed
to carry messages to kings and officials. A trusted
runner was usually on hand during warfare, ready
to carry tidings to the king or emperor.

A battle was in progress between King David's
fighting men and a large army conscripted by his
own son Absalom, who was in rebellion against him.
It was a serious and sad situation, for David loved
Absalom in spite of his treasonous attempt to usurp

the throne. In fact, David gave specific instructions to his men: "For my sake, be sure that Absalom comes back unharmed."

During the fighting, the king waited anxiously at the gate of a nearby city. The battle was soon over. The king's army was victorious, but Absalom was dead. While riding his mule in the heat of the battle, Absalom's head had caught in the branches of a tree.

Joab, the army commander, now needed a runner to carry news to David. It was a good-news, bad-news report—not an easy assignment. A trusted Ethiopian runner was ready, but another fellow, Ahimaaz, who was a young priest and a personal friend of the king, pestered Joab for the job. "Let me run to the king and tell him the good news!" he implored.

"No," Joab responded. "It is not all *good* news." But Ahimaaz was insistent.

"I don't care, let me run." And off he went.

The young priest proved to be a fast runner and overtook the Ethiopian by going a different route. Arriving breathless before the king, he shared the news of victory. David nodded, but quickly asked, "Is Absalom safe?"

Ahimaaz was perplexed by the question and could not answer it. "I saw a huge ruckus just as I started out," he said, "but I don't know what it was about." Soon the Ethiopian arrived with the answer that David wanted but feared to hear. He wept long and bitterly for the son he loved.

How often are we guilty of running with the wrong message or half the truth?

Lord, running may not be my cup of tea,
but I want to use whatever abilities
I have to serve You.

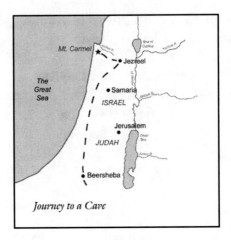

Journey to a Cave

Learn More

Mount Carmel is not a single peak, but a mountain range of limestone, reaching a maximum elevation of 1,500 feet.

Jezreel was the site of the royal palace of Ahab and Jezebel. By this time, it had replaced the town of Samaria as the capital of the kingdom of Israel.

Read More

Read 1 Kings 18:16-46 for the amazing story of Elijah on Mount Carmel, and then read 1 Kings 19:1-18 for the other half of Elijah's rollercoaster ride. Depression results from many different causes. Which of the following may have contributed to Elijah's depression? How might any of these contribute to our own "down" times?

- A rapid succession of exciting events
- Physical exhaustion and lack of sleep
- Threatening situations, including physical dangers and financial problems
- Feelings of hopelessness or inadequacy
- Loneliness
- Anxiety about health issues

2 0

Journey to a Cave

Be still, and know that I am God.
                    —Psalm 46:10 (NIV)

*H*IS LIFE WAS spectacular. Elijah, the "prophet of fire," moved like a crackling fireball through the landscape of ancient Israel. Delivering thundering messages from the Almighty, he electrified the heart of King Ahab, met the challenge of insidious Baal worship head on, performed incredible miracles through the power of Jahweh, and brought an entire nation to its knees in a single day of decision. Other prophets in the Bible merely died, but Elijah left the stage in a spectacular happening described as a "chariot of fire."

The climactic event of Elijah's life was a drama-filled day on Mount Carmel, where the prophet summoned the forces of evil: 850 priests of Baal and Asherah, ready to defend their gods. As the people looked on, Elijah issued an awesome challenge between Baal and God Almighty. The drama ended with a consuming fire from heaven, the slaughter of the evil priests, and the arrival of a great rainstorm that broke a three-year drought.

What a prophet! Yet the close of the event triggered a dark valley experience for Elijah. At the day's end, as Elijah ran ahead of Ahab's chariot in a drenching rainstorm, the adrenaline surging through his body, he finally came to a panting stop at the gates of Jezreel. Suddenly, it was all over. The shouting had died, the crowd was gone, and Elijah was just a cold, wet, lonely man with a death threat over his head.

Engulfed by weariness and fear, Elijah ran southward from the scene to the desert beyond Beersheba. There he hid in a cave, mentally and physically exhausted. "I've had enough," he said. "Just let me die." In that moment of despair, God came to his servant. In a dramatic replay of his life, the prophet experienced in rapid succession a mighty whirlwind, an earthquake, and a roaring fire. But it was not until all the noise and fury was gone and the silence returned that God communicated with Elijah through a "still, small voice."

Of course, God is present in the high points of our lives, but He is also there when we feel empty and afraid, when we take our journeys into the caves of discouragement and depression. It is during these times that we must listen for the "still, small voice" of our caring Father.

Lord, help me remember that You will never leave me nor forsake me.

Journey for Healing

Learn More

The old city of Damascus has been the capital of Syria for at least 3,000 years. Syria (or Aram, as it was then known) was a rising power at the time of Naaman and a thorn in the side of Israel. Naaman's journey took him to the city of Samaria, which was the capital of the kingdom of Israel until the Assyrians took the city during the eighth century B.C. Naaman mistakenly believed that he would find the prophet Elisha in Samaria, but at that time Elisha lived several miles to the north in the town of Dothan.

Read More

Read the story of Naaman in 2 Kings 5:1-18. In ancient times, leprosy was considered a scourge, much the way AIDS is regarded in our day. Do we sometimes treat the "lepers" in our society any differently from the way the king of Israel responded to Naaman's plea for help?

2 1

Journey for Healing

Naaman was the commander of the Syrian army....Naaman was a brave soldier, but he had leprosy.

—2 Kings 5:1 (CEV)

*N*AAMAN SUFFERED FROM leprosy, and he had learned through the captive servant girl who worked for his wife that there was a prophet somewhere in Israel who might cure him. Now there were just two choices available for the Syrian army commander: He could take a trip to neighboring Israel—enemy territory—in the hope of finding a cure, or he could stay at home and watch his body slowly and painfully waste away until he died.

Although it was a journey Naaman wished he did not have to take, he chose the first option. So he set off, accompanied by an entourage loaded with gifts and a letter of reference addressed to the king of Israel, which read, "With this letter I am sending my servant Naaman to you so that you may cure him of his leprosy." Predictably, the Israelite king was not impressed. Standing before him was a military leader of an enemy nation who probably deserved his affliction.

"Go away!" he said. "I can't help you."

Discouraged, Naaman turned toward home. But God had something different planned for the Syrian commander. A messenger arrived and directed him to the home of Elisha the prophet at Dothan. Arriving there, Naaman anticipated having an audience with the man of God, but there was only a cryptic message: "Go, wash yourself seven times in the Jordan, and your flesh will be restored and you will be cleansed."

Naaman felt angry and insulted. Any fool knew that bathing your skin in water did nothing for leprosy. And bathing in the Jordan? It was just a sluggish stream compared to the clear, fast-flowing rivers of Syria and Lebanon.

"Come on, you guys. We're going home."

Fortunately, Naaman's servants persuaded their commander to give the Jordan treatment a try, and it worked, completely. The commander arrived home clean, cured, and convicted that there was a living God out there who cared about him.

God sometimes works in strange and unpredictable ways. We must be always open to His leading.

Lord, help me to surrender my stubborn will to You. I need to be ready to do it Your way.

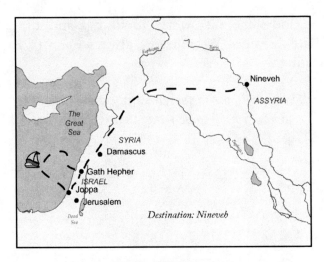

Destination: Nineveh

Learn More

Jonah lived in the village of Gath Hepher (see 2 Kings 14:25), located about five miles from Nazareth. He lived during the time when King Jeroboam II ruled the northern kingdom of Israel.

Nineveh was the capital of the Assyrian Empire, located north of Babylon on the eastern bank of the Tigris River. The walls of Nineveh had a circumference of eight miles. Excavations have uncovered the great palace of Sennacherib, whose military campaigns included the destruction of the city of Babylon in 689 B.C. and the siege of Jerusalem. Jonah's journey from his hometown to Nineveh would have taken him more than 700 miles away.

Read More

Jonah is the only book of Scripture that ends with a question: "Should I not be concerned about that great city?" (Jonah 4:11). God put the question to Jonah, and it tells us something about the concern that He has for His entire creation. He still calls individuals to travel to remote and isolated places where people have desperate needs.

Destination: Nineveh

One day, the Lord spoke to Jonah son of Amittai. He said, "Go to Nineveh, that great city, and speak out against it; I am aware how wicked its people are." Jonah, however, set out in the opposite direction in order to get away from the Lord.
—Jonah 1:1-3 (TEV)

*W*HEN JONAH STUMBLED down to the docks at Joppa and enquired about a passage on a ship, he probably didn't have a particular destination in mind. "Just get me on a ship going to the end of the world—Italy or Africa, it doesn't matter."

He found a Phoenician trading vessel that was sailing for Tarshish, far away in Spain. That was about as close as you could get to the end of the world, for it was common knowledge that somewhere in the vast ocean west of Spain the earth came to an abrupt end and ships were swept over the edge into oblivion. Jonah paid the fare and climbed on board.

The reluctant prophet thought he was running away from God, but really he was running away from himself. When confronted with the task of preaching God's word to an enemy nation that he hated and feared, he decided to go in the opposite direction. Did he really believe he could ignore God's command and relax on a distant shore? After a couple of sleepless nights, tossing and turning in his ship-board bunk, he was overcome with depression.

Jonah's Mediterranean cruise came to an abrupt end with a violent storm, followed by a smelly submarine ride inside the belly of a great fish. By the time Jonah stepped on land again, he was ready to do what God had asked of him. After showering and putting on clean clothes, he set out for Nineveh.

It's possible that Jonah's incredible story reached Nineveh before he did. If so, what an opening for an evangelistic campaign! "Come and hear the man who was swallowed by a great fish and survived!" Did Jonah tell his story to the Ninevites? Scripture doesn't tell us, but we know that the whole city came out to hear the reluctant prophet and that they heeded the warning.

It's really not hard to share personal stories, but far too often, like Jonah, we run away from the opportunity.

I don't have a dramatic experience like Jonah's to tell, but I can share how Jesus has impacted my life.

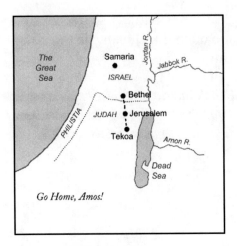

Go Home, Amos!

Learn More

Bethel (literally "the House of God") was the place where Jacob, when fleeing from his brother Esau, was given a vision of a ladder linking earth with heaven (see Gen. 28:10-17). Centuries later, when Israel was divided into two kingdoms, the northern king, Jeroboam, chose Bethel as a temple site, partly to divert his subjects from the temple in Jerusalem. Since Bethel was located at the southern boundary of Jeroboam's kingdom, it was also a strong frontier-fortress town.

Tekoa was a wilderness area south of Bethlehem, where the land dropped away precipitously to the Dead Sea. Agriculture there included sheepherding, growing grapes on terraced slopes, and cultivation of sycamore figs in the valleys.

Read More

Read how God called a simple, uneducated shepherd to be his spokesperson in these selections from the book of Amos: 1:1-2; 2:6-16; 7:7-17; and 9:11-15. In our human judgment, Amos would be the wrong kind of person to be sent to the "uppity folks" in Israel, but God's criteria are often very different from our own.

23

Go Home, Amos!

I'm not a prophet! And I wasn't trained to be a prophet.
I am a shepherd, and I take care of fig trees. But the
Lord told me to leave my herds and preach to the
people of Israel.

—Amos 7:14-15 (CEV)

AMOS WAS ONE of the more colorful prophets of Old Testament times. A simple shepherd, he kept his flocks near Tekoa, located south of Bethlehem. In those days Israel was split into two independent nations. The 10 northern tribes comprised the kingdom of Israel, which was a wealthy trading nation of merchants. The southern kingdom of Judah, where Amos lived, was small and rural, and regarded as inferior by the affluent northerners.

Amos' life was a hard one. Being semi-nomadic, he dressed in rough clothing, slept in a rustic hut, and had to contend with cold damp winters, summer droughts, and wild animals. Sheepherding was regarded as a lowly occupation, but it bred rugged men who placed their trust in the God who ruled the seasons.

It was a surprise when God called a sheepherder from Judah to be His spokesman to the well-heeled, sophisticated citizens of the northern kingdom. Amos responded immediately, leaving his flock in the care of another shepherd and journeying northward to Bethel, where crowds flocked to Jeroboam's temple to worship golden calves. When Amos arrived, he spoke God's messages with boldness. These were messages aimed at social injustice, and they flowed with the colorful vocabulary of an agricultural labourer.

"Hear this word, you cows of Bashan! You sell the righteous for silver and the needy for a pair of sandals! You trample on the heads of the poor like you trample the dust! I will crush you as a cart crushes everything in its path when loaded with grain."

The priests at Bethel did not like the words of the hillbilly prophet. "Get out, you seer!" one priest named Amaziah shouted. "Go back to the land of Judah. Earn your bread there and do your prophesying there. Don't show your face here again. This is the king's chapel and a royal shrine."

Amos' response was from God: "Now listen to what the Lord says: 'Israel will certainly go into exile, away from their native land.'" Less than 50 years later, the armies of Assyria came down from the north and carried the Israelites into captivity.

God is love, but sometimes it has to be tough love.

Lord, help me listen to Your words and warnings and be willing to respond.

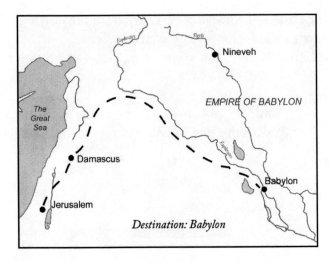

Destination: Babylon

Learn More

The city of Babylon was perhaps the mightiest metropolis of the ancient world and already more than 1,000 years old when Nebuchadnezzar conquered the Assyrians and established it as his capital. It was a large and beautiful city, surrounded by a wall more than 10 miles long and 140 feet thick. From the Ishtar Gate with its 575 enameled dragons, bulls, and lions, the main thoroughfare led past the lavishly decorated palace of the king to the Temple of Marduk. Archaeologists have uncovered the foundations of an old terraced pyramid, or ziggurat, which may have had its origin as the Tower of Babel.

Read More

You can read about the fall of Jerusalem in 2 Chronicles 36:5-21. The Jewish exiles in Babylon were undoubtedly in a state of shock and anxiety. We live in a time when migration and movement of people from one country and culture to another has become commonplace. What responsibilities do we as Christians have toward immigrants who come to make our communities their new home?

Destination: Babylon

By the rivers of Babylon we sat and wept when we remembered Zion. There on the poplars we hung our harps, for there our captors asked us for songs, our tormentors demanded songs of joy; they said, "Sing us one of the songs of Zion!" How can we sing the songs of the Lord while in a foreign land?
—Psalm 137:1-4 (NIV)

*I*F YOU HAVE ever spent time in a country where the culture is different from your own, you can empathize with the Jewish captives in Babylon who were pining for their homeland. Submerged in grief, they hung their harps on the riverbank poplars. When curious onlookers sought to comfort them by asking to hear some of their religious songs, the strangers were sullen and unresponsive. "How can we sing the songs of Zion in a foreign land?" they wailed.

Generations of Jews had received warnings about their idolatrous behaviour. Prophets plead, cajoled, and threatened them. "Unless you repent," they had said, "your holy city, Jerusalem, will be destroyed and you will be exiled to a foreign land." But generation after generation ignored the warnings.

So the unthinkable happened. Even before Nebuchadnezzar's coronation, he marched the king of Judah to Babylon. Accompanying him were some of the Jewish elite, including a young man named Daniel and his friends. But that was only the beginning. Later, the armies of Babylon came and destroyed Jerusalem, turned Solomon's magnificent temple into a rubble heap, and dragged thousands more Jews into captivity. Men, women, and children endured a forced march across the desert to the Babylonian heartland between the Tigris and Euphrates rivers.

After the trauma of the invasion and the forced desert march, the exiles had to face severe culture shock as they found themselves in an alien society. Everything around them seemed hostile: the dress, the customs of the people, the pagan temples. The captives were shattered, heartbroken, and dispirited.

Against this backdrop we have the contrasting story of Daniel and his three friends. Unlike the rest of their countrymen, they adopted a positive mindset, refusing to be devastated by their situation. Three times a day Daniel prayed by his open window, a clear witness to his Babylonian neighbors. Although he and his friends were suspended in an alien culture, they kept their faith and serenity. Zion might be a thousand miles away, in ruins, but its songs were alive in their hearts.

Wherever we live or travel, we must keep hope alive in our hearts.

Lord, help me to find moments of joy in every circumstance.

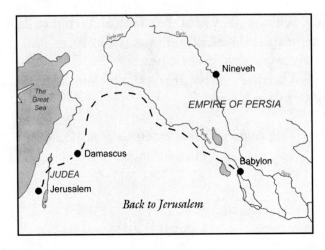

Back to Jerusalem

Learn More

Excavation of the old city of Jerusalem has been plagued by difficulties. This is partly due to the fact that the site is cumbered by modern buildings, but also because the city was besieged, captured, or destroyed in whole or in part more than 40 times. However, archaeologists have been able to sink shafts in the old temple area and tunnel under some existing structures. Among the significant discoveries they found is a 100-ton cornerstone of Solomon's temple and King Hezekiah's water conduit (see 2 Kings 20:20).

Read More

The book of Ezra provides an account of how the exiles rebuilt the altar at Jerusalem and began the construction of a new temple (see Ezra 3). Also described is the return of the exiles, with detailed lists of families and their numbers (see Ezra 2). Many families were missing from the lists because significant numbers of Jews chose to remain in the comforts of Babylonia and not return to their homeland. Is it possible for us to also feel too comfortable in our spiritual state and be unwilling to move forward on our spiritual journey?

Back to Jerusalem

When I say of Cyrus, "He is my shepherd," he will
certainly do as I say; and Jerusalem will be rebuilt
and the Temple restored, for I have spoken it.
                              —Isaiah 44:28 (TLB)

𝓘T HAD BEEN nearly 70 years since
Nebuchadnezzar made his foray into the Jewish
state, taking thousands of Jews into captivity and
leaving towns and cities in ruins. Times had been
hard for the exiles, as they had been separated from
their homeland and their beloved Jerusalem. But
now the time had come for them to go home.

A new generation of Israelites would have the
opportunity to make a new start. The empire of
Babylon had ended its time on the world stage,
and a foreign monarch, King Cyrus, had taken the

throne. The age of the Persian Empire had begun. Within months of taking office, Cyrus announced the end of the Jewish captivity and permitted all who wanted to return to their homeland to do so. He even allowed them to build a new temple, replacing the one that had been destroyed by the Babylonian invaders. Cyrus instructed the returning exiles to take with them the precious items that had been removed from the old temple and placed in storage in Babylon.

It was an exciting day for the exiles. Under the leadership of Zerubbabel, thousands of Israelites packed their goods and formed a great caravan to cross the desert and return to their ancestral homeland. Although it was discouraging for them upon their return to find their villages and towns in ruins, or occupied by foreign peoples, they took courage and began the task of remaking their future.

Zerubbabel led the rebuilding effort in Jerusalem. The people built an altar on the site of the old temple and offered sacrifices of praise and thanksgiving to the Lord. The new temple would take years to complete, but the completion of the new foundation was an occasion for joyous celebration and great shouts of praise to the Lord.

The excitement was tempered by the sadness of some of the elderly members who remembered the magnificence of Solomon's temple and the size of its foundations, but their weeping was drowned out by the joyful singing and shouting of the people. This was not a time to think or talk about faded glory. A new day had dawned for Israel. Now was the time to forget past failures and celebrate new beginnings.

Disappointment and failure are part of our lives. Praise God for new beginnings.

Please, Lord, revive our hearts and renew our commitment.

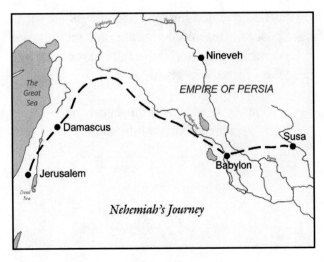

Nehemiah's Journey

Learn More

Susa, also known as Shushan in biblical times, was already a very old city at the time of the Jewish captivity. Situated at the foot of the mountains about 200 miles east of Babylon, Susa was the capital city of several consecutive empires. It was destroyed by the Assyrians but rebuilt by Nebuchadnezzar, who established it as a winter capital. Later, Susa became the capital of the Persian Empire, and an elaborate palace covering 123 acres was built there. Daniel spent the later years of his life in Susa, and Esther was queen there during the reign of the Persian king Xerxes.

Read More

Nehemiah's first-person account of his leadership is inspiring. Read Nehemiah 1–2 and catch the excitement as he awakens energy in the people of Jerusalem. Then read Nehemiah 6:1-16, where he describes how the wall was completed in spite of enemy attempts to sabotage the work. Nehemiah asked God to strengthen his hands (see Neh. 6:9) and he felt God's hand upon him (see Neh. 2:8).

Nehemiah's Journey

*During the month of Chislev in the twentieth year
that Artaxerxes ruled Persia, I was in his fortress
city of Susa, when my brother Hanani came with
some men from Judah. So I asked them about
the Jews who had escaped from being captives
in Babylon. I also asked them about the city of
Jerusalem.*

— Nehemiah 1:1-2 (CEV)

*M*ANY YEARS HAD passed since Zerubbabel led
a company of exiles home from Babylon with
the task of rebuilding Jerusalem. Among the Jews
remaining in the Persian Empire was a man named
Nehemiah. Although he served in the Persian court
as the king's cupbearer, his heart was far away in the
land of his fathers.

Growing up in Babylon and now living in the royal capital of Susa, Nehemiah could only imagine what Jerusalem must have looked like after the restoration. He was surrounded by the opulence of palaces, gardens, and temples, so he pictured a city with strong walls and a dazzling temple. When his brother Hanani arrived from Jerusalem for a visit, Nehemiah plied him with questions. Was everyone doing well in the homeland? What about Jerusalem, and the new temple?

Nehemiah was stunned by his brother's response. "The exile survivors are in bad shape. Conditions are appalling. The wall of Jerusalem is still rubble, and the city gates are still cinders. And as for the temple...well, the old men say it compares poorly with Solomon's magnificent edifice."

Nehemiah wept on hearing this, and his countenance was still downcast when he brought wine to the king several days later. "Is something bothering you?" the king asked. Nehemiah was ready with an answer. "I feel sad because the city where my ancestors are buried is in ruins, and its gates have been burned down." He paused. "Sir, if it's all right with you, please send me back to Judah so I can rebuild the city where my ancestors are buried." King Artaxerxes graciously granted Nehemiah's request.

Later, arriving in Jerusalem, Nehemiah found an unprotected city with broken-down walls and towers in ruins. After a tour of inspection, he challenged the city officials, saying, "Jerusalem is truly in a mess.

We must rebuild the wall." Everyone rallied around the new leader. With the blessing of God, and in spite of enemy attempts to sabotage the work, the wall of Jerusalem was rebuilt in just 52 days!

God is empowered when we give our abilities to Him.

Lord, I'm willing to be Your hands and feet.

SHEEP AND SHEPHERDS IN THE BIBLE

There are numerous Bible passages that feature sheep and shepherds. Here are several for your reading:

- **Genesis 29:1-12.** Jacob arrives at Haran after a long journey from Canaan. After speaking with the shepherds, he meets a shepherdess named Rachel. For Jacob, it was probably love at first sight.
- **2 Samuel 12:1-10.** The prophet Nathan is sent by the Lord to rebuke King David, who had arranged to have Uriah killed in battle so that he could marry his wife, Bathsheba. You will appreciate Nathan's creativity in telling the story about a little ewe lamb. Our sins can cause deep hurt to others.
- **Psalm 23.** This is one of the most loved chapters in the Bible: the Shepherd Psalm. Try reading it in a contemporary English version.
- **Isaiah 53:1-8.** This is a prophetic passage that foretells the suffering of Christ, who was led as a lamb to the slaughter.
- **Matthew 18:12-14.** Jesus tells His hearers a parable about the shepherd who, when one lost sheep wanders away, leaves the other 99 to go in search of it. That lost sheep could have been me.
- **John 1:29-34.** John the Baptist introduces Jesus to the crowds at the Jordan baptismal site, proclaiming Him to be the Lamb of God who takes away the sin of the world.
- **John 10:1-18.** Jesus introduces Himself as the Good Shepherd.
- **Revelation 5:6-13.** In this passage, we are given a glimpse of the victory celebration in heaven after Jesus' death, resurrection, and ascension. Worthy is the Lamb!

Journey of a Shepherd

*Because the Lord is my Shepherd, I have everything
I need! He lets me rest in the meadow grass and
leads me beside the quiet streams.*
                                    —Psalm 23:1-2 (TLB)

*G*OD MUST LOVE sheep, because sheep and
shepherds are all through the Bible, beginning with the story of Abel's lamb in Genesis and
concluding with Christ as the victorious Lamb in
Revelation. Several Scriptures liken people to sheep,
and not always in a flattering way.

If there is one quality that a sheep farmer must
possess, it is patience. Sheep have a reputation
for wandering away on their own and getting into
hopeless predicaments. In New Zealand, where

sheep outnumber people 10 to 1, the farmers would have given up long ago if they did not have those amazing border collies to control the flocks.

In one of Jesus' stories, He tells about a sheep that wanders away and becomes lost. The creature is helpless, its situation hopeless. Left alone in the wilderness when night falls, the animal will likely become food for a hungry wolf. The shepherd, corralling his sheep at the end of a weary day, counts them and discovers that one is missing. It would be easy for him to write off the loss as bad luck—as one of the risks of sheep herding—but the shepherd will not do that. Leaving his flock in the care of a family member or hired hand, he lights a lantern and goes out into the night to find the lost one. He may spend most of the night searching until he finds the sheep, and then carry the cold and trembling animal home on his shoulders, rejoicing that the lost has been found.

The picture of Christ as the Good Shepherd is one of the most beautiful in Scripture. Whether we like to admit it or not, we are much like sheep—stupid and prone to wander away from the protection and care of our Master. Lost and totally helpless, we are potential fodder for a "roaring lion, seeking whom he may devour"(1 Peter 5:8). We are saved only because our caring Shepherd takes the journey into the wilderness of sin and carries us back to safety and home.

Lord, I pray for each precious member of my family. Please be my Shepherd, too.

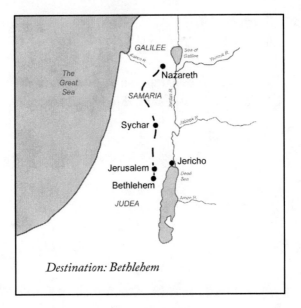

Destination: Bethlehem

Learn More

The "royal city" of Bethlehem was given that name because King David was born there, and it was predicted that the Messiah would come from there as well (see Micah 5:2). The town is located about six miles south of Jerusalem. The journey from Nazareth to Bethlehem, if using the direct route through Samaria, would have been about 70 miles and taken about one week.

Read More

Luke's account of the birth of Jesus is well known and often read aloud during each Christmas season. Read Luke 2:1-20, and try to imagine the trauma of the journey for Mary and Joseph. So many things seemed to go wrong for them at this time. Perhaps we can find courage from the story when circumstances beyond our control mess up our own carefully laid plans. Most often, this seems to happen with travel plans.

28

Destination: Bethlehem

*In those days Caesar Augustus issued a decree that a
census should be taken of the entire Roman world....
So Joseph also went up from the town of Nazareth in
Galilee to Judea, to Bethlehem the town of David.*
— Luke 2:1,4 (NIV)

FOR JOSEPH, IT was the year when everything
went wrong.

The quiet life of the Nazareth carpenter had
been shattered by a series of devastating events. It
began with the shocking discovery that his fiancée
was expecting a baby that was not his. That was bad
enough, though Joseph clung desperately to Mary's
simple trust in him and the angel's remarkable
testimony. What they both anticipated was a quiet
birth in the simple privacy of a Nazareth home. But
it was not to be.

One day, the village buzzed with an announce-
ment from Rome that a world census was to take
place at a specified time. Everyone had to go to
his or her family "home" town to register. When
Joseph heard the news, he was mortified. The
census coincided with the projected birth date,
which meant that he and Mary had to travel a
great distance to the old royal city of Bethlehem
to register.

The long trip on a donkey was extremely arduous
for Mary. Joseph should not have been surprised
when she complained of abdominal cramps as they
stumbled through the town gate into the crowded
streets of Bethlehem. This was not the way they
wanted it to happen. Suddenly, it became critical to
find a comfortable room where they could prepare
for the new-life event.

The final blow came with the realization that
there was not even one vacancy in the overcrowded
town. A desperate Joseph finally accepted the offer of
an innkeeper's stable, dirty and smelly as it was. The
infant born there that night was no ordinary child,
but the distraught father must have wondered why
every circumstance had conspired against him. He
was too mind-weary just then to recall the ancient
writing of Micah the prophet, specifying Bethlehem
as the birthplace of the Messiah.

Before the long night ended, shepherds from the
surrounding hills were crowding into the dimly lit
stable, worshiping the newborn as the wondering
parents looked on. Today, the world celebrates the

night of Joseph's trauma. The time when everything went wrong for him became the moment when everything turned out right for all of us. Wonderfully right!

Thank You, dear Jesus, for Your incredible love and sacrifice for us.

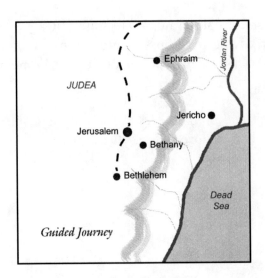

Guided Journey

Learn More

The wise men found Mary and Joseph with the child Jesus living in a house in Bethlehem (see Matt. 2:11). The evidence suggests that Jesus might have been about two years old when the wise men came to find him. Because Joseph came from the royal line of David, it is possible that he owned land in Bethlehem, which may explain why he and Mary did not return to Nazareth after the birth. Shortly thereafter, they fled to Egypt when King Herod ordered the killing of all boys in Bethlehem who were two years of age and under (see Matt. 2:16). After the death of Herod, the family returned from Egypt and made their home in Nazareth.

Read More

The visit of the wise men is told in Matthew 2:1-12. These men travelled the long distance to Palestine with expectation and faith. In our journey through life, we sometimes fail to see evidence of our Lord's leading, but we will always have the "star" of God's Word and the Holy Spirit as our trustworthy guide.

29

Guided Journey

After Jesus was born in Bethlehem in Judea, during the time of King Herod, wise men from the East came to Jerusalem and asked, "Where is the one who has been born king of the Jews? We saw his star in the east and have come to worship him."
—Matthew 2:1-2 (NIV)

WE KNOW VERY little about the wise men. Known as Magi, they were experts in the study of the stars and were perhaps the astronomers of their time. Tradition holds that they were three in number and were kings from as far away as India, but there is no clear evidence to support this claim.

The story is all about following a star. These scholarly and highly respected men became excited when a new star appeared in their night sky. They decided that its sudden appearance must signify that an extraordinary event would occur—perhaps the birth of the long-promised Messiah for the Jewish people.

When the wise men announced to their friends and families that they were leaving home to follow a star to an undetermined location, they might have been denounced as the "three fools." Who else would leave the comforts of home to go on a pilgrimage with an unknown destination, an uncertain event, carrying expensive gifts for an unknown person, and with just a star for direction?

But go they did, across hot and cold deserts and dangerous places, travelling for weeks and perhaps months as they followed the heavenly sign. At last they arrived in Jerusalem, expectant and enquiring, only to find that no one knew anything about a recent extraordinary event such as the birth of the Messiah. Finally, they wound up in the court of King Herod, who consulted the priests and historians. The Scriptures, these men said, pointed to Bethlehem as the birthplace of the Messiah. King Herod seemed ecstatic with the information and asked the wise men to come back and tell him what they found. But the king's ecstasy was more like savagery, and fortunately the visitors were wise enough to listen to the voice of God. After finding and worshiping the child Jesus, they headed homeward by a different route. Mission accomplished.

There is nothing wrong with following your star. Just keep in touch with God and be ready to modify your plans as He directs.

Lord, please be my guide when I travel to far away places.

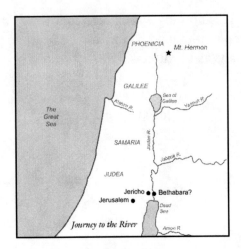

Journey to the River

Learn More

The Jordan River is the lifeblood of Israel, but it is also important for the nearby countries of Syria and Jordan. Fed from tributaries coming from Lebanon and Mount Hermon, it descends rapidly to the Sea of Galilee at 690 feet below sea level. From there it meanders southward to the Dead Sea, which is the lowest point on earth at 1,350 feet below sea level. Heavy use of the river by three countries has reduced the flow of water into the Dead Sea, causing it to shrink in size. In 2007, Friends of the Earth named the Jordan as one of the world's most endangered ecological sites because of excessive water diversion and pollution.

John 1:28 names Bethabara as one place where John the Baptist conducted baptisms. The location is uncertain, but it may have been on the east bank, opposite Jericho.

Read More

Matthew 3:13-17 records the event of Jesus' baptism at the Jordan. Also read John 1:19-34 for the testimony of John the Baptist, who was chosen by God to prepare the way for the Messiah.

30

Journey to the River

*At that time Jesus came from Nazareth in Galilee
and was baptized by John in the Jordan.*
—Mark 1:9 (NIV)

I AM GLAD that Jesus did not journey to the shores of the Dead Sea for His baptism. The Salt Sea, which is its biblical name, receives its water from the Jordan and several desert watercourses but has no outlet. For that reason, its waters are highly saline and stagnant. It is a sea of death.

I'm also glad that Jesus did not choose a spring-fed pool in the hills of Palestine for His baptism. If he had, the place would certainly have become a shrine where holy water could be bottled and dispensed to pilgrims at high prices, or where millions would congregate to bathe and imagine themselves cleansed of defilement.

No, Jesus travelled down from Nazareth to the ever-flowing waters of the Jordan, where John the Baptist was preaching to crowds that came to hear and respond to his call for heart-searching and repentance. It was there that Jesus received baptism.

Whatever you think about the Jordan, it is not just any old river. The Jordan was (and still is) the lifeblood of Palestine and the desert lands to the east, but there is something quite special about it. The course of the Jordan flows along one segment of an amazing geological fault known as the Great Rift Valley, a 6,000-mile-long fissure that extends all the way from Lebanon down through East Africa to Mozambique.

I am glad that my Savior chose the flowing river for His baptism. From Him alone flows the spiritual lifeblood that energizes the Christian and heals the great rift that sin has brought to this planet. Jesus Christ is the fountain of living water, the cleansing stream that washes away our sins. Every individual seeking soul cleansing must make the journey to that river.

Lord, please wash me in the cleansing stream
of Your righteousness.

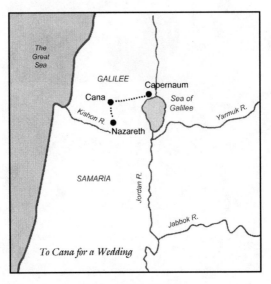

The Great Sea

GALILEE

Cana

Capernaum

Sea of Galilee

Kishon R.

Yarmuk R.

Nazareth

SAMARIA

Jordan R.

Jabbok R.

To Cana for a Wedding

Learn More

It is believed that an archaeological site known as Kfar-Cana, located about five miles north of Nazareth, is the village where Jesus performed His first miracle. Cana dates back to the time when the Israelites entered Canaan and divided the new territory by lot (see Josh. 14–19). Scholars believe that Cana is located on the same site as Et-Kazim, which is mentioned in Joshua 19:13 as being the portion of the land that fell to the sons of Zebulun. In the excavations at Kfar-Cana, archaeologists have found several stone water jars of the type that would have been used at a wedding.

Read More

Read John 1:43-49 and 2:1-11. The first recorded marriage took place in Eden, when God created Eve and brought her to Adam. Since marriage was ordained and blessed by God, should we be surprised that Jesus' first public act of His ministry was participation in a wedding? We must not lose sight of marriage as a sacred institution.

31

To Cana for a Wedding

*Three days later Mary, the mother of Jesus, was at
a wedding feast in the village of Cana in Galilee.
Jesus and His disciples had also been invited and
were there.*

—John 2:1-2 (CEV)

*J*ESUS' FAMILY HOME was the village of
Nazareth, located near the western shore
of Lake Galilee. One day, Jesus appeared on the
lakeshore at Capernaum, where He called His first
disciples—Peter, Andrew, James and John—from
their fishing boats. The following day He called
another young man, Philip, who could hardly wait
to share the exciting news with his friend Nathaniel.

"Listen, we've found the one Moses and the prophets wrote about! It's Jesus of Nazareth, Joseph's son."

Nathaniel's hometown was Cana, a village seven miles north of Nazareth, so he knew the area well. His reaction to Philip's news was immediate.

"What? Nazareth! Can anything good come from there?"

"You come and see," urged Philip. He led his friend to Christ, and Nathaniel was quickly convinced that Jesus was indeed the promised Messiah. "You are the Son of God!" he declared. Both young men became disciples.

Nathaniel likely shared his excitement with his family and friends back in Cana. Just three days later a wedding took place there, and Jesus, His mother, and His new disciples were all invited guests. Jewish wedding feasts went on for days, so it is not surprising that the wine ran out before the celebration ended. When Jesus heard about the problem, He performed His first miracle, converting jars of water into a beverage of superb quality.

So the first public event that Jesus attended in company with His disciples was a family social event—a wedding. His chosen followers discovered that their new teacher was not a recluse who would lead them into monastic isolation, as they might have expected. Instead, their training and ministry would be thoroughly people-oriented, in keeping with Christ's salvation imperative.

The miracle of the wine must have also convinced those disciples that their Master was not just an extraordinary human being but the Messiah, the God-Man invested with miracle-working power and authority. His teaching would be as refreshing as new wine when compared with the old, insipid traditions of the time.

The story is also good news for us today. God is interested in every facet of our lives, our joys and our journeys.

I thank You, Lord, that I can confide in You.

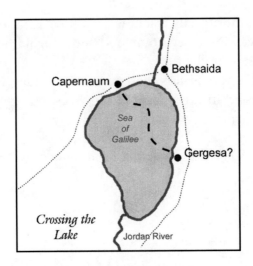

Capernaum ● | ● Bethsaida

Sea of Galilee

● Gergesa?

Crossing the Lake

Jordan River

Learn More

In Christ's day, the town of Capernaum was an important commercial center of the northern Galilee region. Rome had a military garrison there with a centurion in charge, as well as a tax agency. One of the tax collectors in the city, Matthew, became a disciple of Jesus. Jesus spent a large part of His ministry in the area and performed many miracles there. He and His disciples probably started their lake crossing at or near Capernaum.

The town of Gergesa (also known as Gadara) was located on the sparsely populated eastern shore of Galilee. Jesus and the disciples' lake voyage ended there, and it was in this vicinity that Jesus healed the demoniac (see Mark 5:1-17).

Read More

Read the account of the storm on Lake Galilee in Mark 4:35-41. Notice the question Jesus asked in verse 40: "Why were you afraid? Don't you have any faith?" (CEV). How does faith and trust operate when we engage in travel by land, air, or water? Do we pray before setting out on a journey?

32

Crossing the Lake

As evening fell, Jesus said to His disciples, "Let's cross to the other side of the lake." So they took Him just as He was and started out, leaving the crowds behind.

—Mark 4:35-36 (TLB)

*A*FTER A LONG day of teaching under the Mediterranean sun, a weary Jesus seeks escape from the demanding multitude. As evening comes, He and His disciples climb on board one of the fishing boats and set off for sparsely inhabited country on the other side of Lake Galilee. The wind is light and the lake calm as night spreads its curtain over the water. With the gentle rocking of the boat in the darkness, the exhausted Jesus is soon sound asleep in the stern of the boat.

It is not unusual for summer storms to funnel down to Galilee from the mountains to the north, bringing violent winds onto the lake. It happens this night as the disciples steer their boat across the black waters. Suddenly, the sails are flapping wildly, the sea is boisterous, and huge waves smash into the bow, overflowing into the boat. These fishermen are accustomed to storms on the lake, but this one is more violent than any they have encountered before. The men are soon drenched with spray and struggling to keep their craft from sinking or capsizing.

In those desperate moments, someone remembers that Jesus came on board with them. Where is their Master? To their amazement, He is still sleeping in the stern of the violently pitching ship. They shake Him awake, shouting to be heard above the storm, "Teacher, don't you care if we drown?"

Roused from slumber, Jesus immediately stands steady in the tossing boat. His words come clearly above the roar of the gale: "Quiet! Be still!" There is a moan in the rigging as the wind dies away. Moments later, the lake is calm once more, a quietness stealing over the water, interrupted only by the cries of astonishment from the men. The voyage ends in tranquility.

When you are feeling frazzled or fatigued, it may be time to take a mini-vacation to the other side of the lake. But be sure to invite Jesus, the peace-giver, to sail with you. Life's storms have a nasty habit of breaking overhead without much warning.

Lord, sometimes my ship encounters rough waters. Please come aboard and take control.

Mountaintops

Mountains of Palestine

Mount Carmel rises abruptly from the Mediterranean and then continues southeastward as a high ridge of limestone for 15 miles. In Elijah's time, Mount Carmel was a center for Baal worship (see 1 Kings 18:19-40).

Mount Gilboa forms part of the northern boundary of the Jezreel Valley. King Saul and his army camped there during his last battle with the Philistines (see 1 Sam. 31:1-3).

Mount Tabor is a high mountain west of Lake Galilee. Some believe that Jesus was transfigured there (see Matt. 17:1-9). Much earlier, Deborah and Barak camped there with an army as they prepared to fight the Canaanites at the Kishon River (see Judg. 4:4-7).

Mount Gerizim was sacred to the Samaritans, who constructed a temple on its summit. Much earlier, Israelite tribes stood on Mount Gerizim and recited the blessings that would result from their obedience to God's laws (see Deut. 27:12).

Mount Ebal is Gerizim's twin, a short distance northward. The Samaritans regarded it as a cursed mountain, since the Israelites stood on that mount and recited curses for disobedience (see Deut. 27:13).

33

Mountaintops

Right away, Jesus made His disciples get into a boat and start back across the lake. But He stayed until He had sent the crowds away. Then He went up on a mountain where He could be alone and pray.
—Matthew 14:22-23 (CEV)

*J*ESUS WAS A lover of mountains. They were His favorite haunts to spend time with His disciples for their training sessions as well as for rest and renewal. Often, He retreated alone to the hills for prayer communication with His Father. Sometimes the solitude was broken when the seeking multitudes found Him there.

Most of us have felt the drawing power of mountains. They amaze us with their grandeur and magnificence. They inspire respect and worship in us, as they did in past ages when people thought of them as dwelling places of the gods and chose them as sites for altars, temples, and shrines. Sometimes mountains frighten us, spewing volcanic fire or releasing destructive avalanches.

I am a lover of mountains. I have climbed dozens of peaks with my friends in eastern Australia, and I always anticipated the excitement of standing on the summits and viewing the world below. Whenever we climbed those mountaintops, it did something special and important for us. It gave us a sense of where we were, where we had come from, and where we were going. Those mountains gave us direction.

We enjoyed those mountain summits for another reason as well. In the distant valleys below were the crowded towns and cities, the busy highways, and the industrial haze. In the clear air of the mountaintops, we were above the pollution, the traffic congestion, and the hustle and bustle of living.

There are interesting spiritual parallels. Each of us needs "mountaintop" experiences to reset our spiritual compass, discover where we are, determine where we have come from, and understand where we ought to be going. But we also need mountaintops for the refreshing times of solitude, the clearer air of reality, the escape from the busyness and stress of our lives, and the opportunity to spend vital moments with our Lord.

I think Jesus needed mountaintop experiences for the very same reasons—to break away from the restless world, spend time with His Father, contemplate His mission, and refocus His vision.

Lord, when I'm travelling and away from home routines, it's easy to neglect my time with You. Wherever I am, lead me to "mountaintop" experiences.

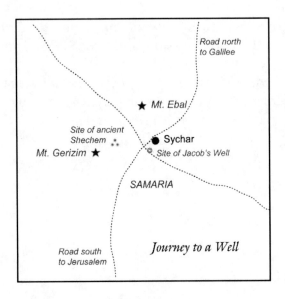

Journey to a Well

Learn More

The Samaritan town of Sychar is mentioned only once in Scripture, in connection with Jesus' journey through Samaria with His disciples. Sychar was located a short distance north of Jacob's Well, near an important crossroads. Some have wondered if Sychar was the site of the ancient town of Shechem (modern Nablus), but archaeologists have identified the ruins of Shechem and believe that Sychar was a mile or two away.

Shechem is the place where Abraham built an altar to the Lord after arriving in Canaan. Later, Jacob purchased a plot of adjacent land and dug the well that is there to this day.

Read More

Read the full story of Jesus and the Samaritan woman in John 4:1-42. Many of the people of Sychar came to believe in Christ because of the woman's testimony. Suppose she had kept it to herself? This story shows us that a personal testimony may be more compelling than a sermon.

Journey to a Well

He had to go through Samaria, and on His way He
came to the town of Sychar. It was near the field
that Jacob had long ago given to his son Joseph.
The well that Jacob had dug was still there, and
Jesus sat down beside it because He was tired from
travelling. It was noon.

—John 4:4-6 (CEV)

*I*T IS NOON on a hot, summer day in the
Samaritan village of Sychar. In the public square,
a handful of merchants drowse at their market stalls.
Most villagers by this time have withdrawn to the
coolness of their mud-brick houses. One woman
with a water pot on her head, however, moves si-
lently and unobtrusively through the streets. Passing

through the village gate, she takes a well-worn path through the grain fields.

Her destination is the Well of Jacob, where women come each day to draw water. They come in the early mornings and cool evenings, but never in the heat of the day. Their trips are social occasions; times to share stories, laugh, and gossip. At midday, the well is a solitary place.

Not today, though. As the woman with the water pot approaches the well, she is startled to see a man there. He is a stranger and—heaven forbid!—a Jew. It is not unusual to see Jews travelling hereabout, as Sychar straddles the road linking Jerusalem with the northern province of Galilee, but Jews despise Samaritans and will speak to a Samaritan woman only if it is necessary to ask for lodging or to buy food. So the woman from the village has nothing to fear. She will just ignore the man, fill her pot, and trudge back to the village.

But it does not turn out that way, for this is no ordinary man but the Christ, the long-promised Messiah. The first surprise is when He asks for a drink of water. That begins a conversation that goes from water to worship and finally to questions that penetrate her soul and reveal the intimacies of her adulterous life. This man is clearly a prophet, and yet more than a prophet.

Abandoning her water pot, the woman hurries back to the village, rousing everyone from their slumber, telling them that the longed-for Messiah has come.

For us, too, Jesus is the well of living water, and no one is denied access to Him.

Our world is still embittered by ethnic hatred and social stigma. Lord, I need to demonstrate Your grace and acceptance.

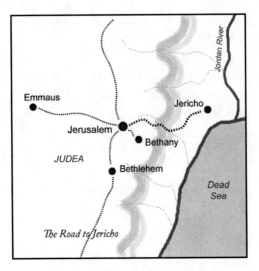

Learn More

Jericho is one of the oldest inhabited towns in the world. Situated in the Jordan Valley about 15 miles from Jerusalem, it is the lowest town on earth at almost 900 feet below sea level. The excavations performed at Jericho have uncovered many remains of this ancient walled city.

Known as the "City of Palms," Jericho contains many historic sites, several of them related to events mentioned in the Bible. Jesus visited Jericho at least once during His ministry (see Luke 18:35-19:10). In New Testament times, the city was the winter capital of Herod the Great and contained many fine buildings, including a hippodrome, a swimming pool, fountains, gardens, and villas. At that time, the city was much closer to the northern shore of the Dead Sea, whose waters have receded over time.

Read More

The narrative of the Good Samaritan is one of Jesus' most-loved and best-known stories. Read Luke 10:25-37. Why did Jesus relate the story? Who is our neighbor?

3 5

The Road to Jericho

A Jew going on a trip from Jerusalem to Jericho was attacked by bandits. They stripped him of his clothes and money and beat him up, and left him lying half dead beside the road....A despised Samaritan came along, and when he saw him, he felt deep pity. Kneeling beside him the Samaritan soothed his wounds with medicine and bandaged them. Then he put the man on his donkey and walked along beside him till they came to an inn, where he nursed him through the night.
—Luke 10:30, 33-34 (TLB)

FROM THE OUTSKIRTS of Jerusalem the road leads eastward, descending through canyons and ravines until it emerges onto the plain at Jericho near the shore of the Dead Sea. Four people are Jericho-bound this morning.

The first traveller may not reach the city alive. A ruthless gang of bandits has done its gruesome work, and he now lies in a pool of blood on the roadside, semi-conscious and half naked.

Enter traveller number two. A priest, a spiritual leader appointed to minister love and compassion to the sin-sick and weary. He pauses to inspect the victim, but with other priorities of time and space, quickly continues his journey.

Traveller number three is a Levite, a teacher of Scripture and religious law. He contemplates the roadside victim, curses the authorities for permitting lawlessness to go unchecked, and then hurries on toward Jericho.

Finally, in the heat of the day, traveller number four arrives, leading a small laden donkey. He is a Samaritan, a foreigner to these parts; despised by the locals, but he has a heart that cares for hurting people.

Imagine that today is your once-in-a-lifetime chance to visit Jericho. The resort by the side of the Salt Sea has swaying palms, a beach, exotic markets, hot tubs, a golf course, and everything else. As you ease your rental car around the curves on the canyon descent, you suddenly encounter a body by the roadside. Is the injured person dead or alive? The crows are already circling in anticipation. But your itinerary is tight, and you are a tourist in a not-too-friendly country. There are strange customs, and a language barrier. You have just seconds to make a decision. You are the "Samaritan."

Lord, give me courage and a heart of love to do my small part in relieving suffering.

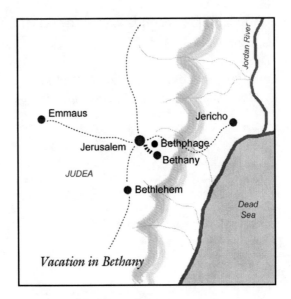

Vacation in Bethany

Learn More

The village of Bethany was the home of Mary, Martha, and Lazarus. The site is now called el-Azariyeh and is situated on the eastern slopes of the Mount of Olives, approximately two miles by road from Jerusalem. We cannot identify the home of the family where Jesus stayed, but among the older ruins is a cave tomb that some believe to have been the tomb of Lazarus.

Near Bethany was the village of Bethphage, which Jesus also visited. It was to Bethphage that He sent His disciples to fetch a donkey for the triumphal procession at the beginning of Passion Week (see Matt. 21:1-2).

Read More

The account of Jesus' visit to Bethany is found in Luke 10:38-42. On that occasion, Martha was overcome with her meal preparation and other responsibilities. Jesus' rebuke to her has something to say to us about dealing with stress in our lives.

Vacation in Bethany

The Lord and His disciples were travelling along and came to a village. When they got there, a woman named Martha welcomed Him in her home.

—Luke 10:38 (CEV)

ONE OF JESUS' favourite places was Bethany, a rural hamlet nestled on a hillside less than an hour's walk from Jerusalem. The village was a haven of rest and relaxation from the noisy crowds and political turmoil of the city.

Jesus' special place in Bethany is a simple, white adobe house built against a narrow lane that winds through the village. The furnishings of the little farmhouse are simple and basic, and the beds are lumpy, but Jesus is always given the best room, its window framed by grapevines opening onto the lane. There, the Master wakes to the morning sounds and smells of the hamlet: the clucking of a hen, the distant braying of a donkey, the unsteady breathing of a bent old woman passing slowly by with a pitcher of water fetched from the village well. There is a mud swallow's nest above the window and the periodic twitter of young birds as the parents bring them their breakfast.

A weary Jesus rests in bed as the village comes to life, enjoying the morning solitude and savouring the aroma of fresh-baked bread wafting in from the outside oven. This is the kind of rejuvenating experience the busy Teacher needs from time to time.

Several times during Jesus' ministry, He took the winding path leading from Jerusalem over the Mount of Olives to His favourite village. His destination was the home of Mary, Martha, and Lazarus, two sisters and a brother who were always ready to welcome the itinerant Christ and to minister lovingly to His needs for rest and sustenance.

There is something important about those visits to Bethany. No one in the history of the universe has ever carried an agenda as momentous as our Lord. His life here on earth was so brief, His ministry so crammed into three short years, His priorities so critical for our salvation. Yet He periodically took time out to travel to an obscure village for a visit with friends. It is a refreshing journey that we all often need to take as well.

Lord, my life is so busy, even with doing good things. Teach me to take "time out" with You.

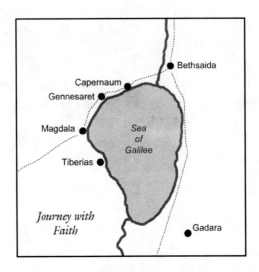

Capernaum
Gennesaret
Bethsaida
Magdala
Sea
of
Galilee
Tiberias
Journey with
Faith
Gadara

Learn More

Capernaum was inhabited for at least 1,000 years. Excavations have uncovered the ruins of a large synagogue constructed from limestone blocks dating from the fourth or fifth century A.D. Underneath the site are the foundations of an even earlier synagogue that may have been built with financial assistance from the centurion whose servant Jesus healed. It was probably the same synagogue in which Jesus worshiped and taught on at least one occasion (see Mark 1:21).

Read More

There are two accounts of the healing of the centurion's servant. Matthew, whose home was Capernaum, was probably present on this occasion and recalled the incident personally (see Matt. 8:5-13), while Luke depended on the recollections of others (see Luke 7:1-10). The essential truth in both accounts is the amazing faith of a Gentile, who believed that Jesus could heal his servant without ever coming to see him or touch him. Have you seen this degree of faith in the lives of some individuals?

37

Journey with Faith

*When Jesus had entered Capernaum, a centurion
came to him, asking for help. "Lord," he said, "my
servant lies at home paralyzed and in terrible
suffering."*

—Matthew 8:5-6 (NIV)

*J*ESUS PERFORMED MUCH of His healing
work in and around Capernaum, a town on
the northern shore of Galilee. It was here that Jesus
called His first disciples from their fishing boats.
During His ministry He visited Capernaum often,
teaching and healing there, and He was loved by the
common people of the town.

Among the residents of Capernaum was a
centurion who was probably in charge of a Roman
garrison stationed there. Unlike the typical soldier

who demonstrated authority in ways that the Jews intensely disliked, this commander developed a cordial relationship with the townspeople, even contributing to the building of their synagogue.

One day as Jesus was walking through the town, accompanied by His disciples and an adoring crowd of townspeople, the centurion approached him. The crowd stepped back respectfully, wondering what a Gentile—even an army captain—wanted with their teacher.

"Master, my servant lies at home sick," the centurion said. "He is paralyzed and in terrible pain."

"I will go and heal him," Jesus responded.

Respectfully, the commander shook his head. "No, sir, I am not worthy to have you come under my roof. Just give the order and my servant will be fine. You see," he explained, "I am a man who takes orders and gives orders. I tell one soldier, 'Go,' and he goes; to another, 'Come,' and he comes; to my slave, 'Do this,' and he does it."

Turning to address the crowd around Him, Jesus exclaimed, "I am telling you the truth, I have not found anyone in Israel with this much faith!" That remark brought a shocked reaction from the crowd of onlookers.

Turning to the centurion, Jesus said, "You can go. Your servant is now well."

Distances of time and place mean nothing to God. Three times during Jesus' ministry, He performed miracles of healing without ever coming near the patient. It is interesting that two of those healings involved Gentile believers!

Jesus is still the healer of souls and bodies. His physical presence is not required. Faith and acceptance of the divine will are the only requirements.

*Lord, give me faith that You will do whatever
is best for me.*

THE LOST SON

Read the story of the lost son in Luke 15:1-2, 11-32. Jesus' story tells us something important about a heavenly Father who longs for us to come home and runs to meet us. The idea of a father running to his children would have seemed preposterous to those listening to Jesus' story. In Jewish society, fathers were not expected to run to anyone, but God cares so much for runaways that He runs to meet them and welcomes them home!

38

Journey from a Far Country

*There was a man who had two sons. The younger
one said to his father, "Father, give me my share of
the estate." So he divided his property between them.
Not long after that, the younger son got together
all he had, set off for a distant country, and there
squandered his wealth in wild living.*
—Luke 15:11-13 (NIV)

THE PARABLE OF the Lost Son is probably
the best known of all of Jesus' stories. It's
a riches-to-rags account of a boy who leaves the
shelter of his home to see the world. Reaching a
distant country, he squanders his money in wild
living before plummeting to the depths of poverty
and depravity.

What point was Jesus trying to make with this story? Christ's audience that day comprised an interesting mixture of people. Sitting in front of Him was a motley group of hated tax collectors and other "sinners." Behind them stood several Pharisees and teachers who were muttering about Jesus' association with the dregs of society, represented by those up in front. Jesus even ate with these outcasts.

Hearing their accusations, Jesus told the story of the lost son who came near to perishing of hunger in the distant country. Miraculously, though, the boy overcame a thousand obstacles and struggled home, where he was welcomed by a loving father but spurned by an angry and uncaring older brother.

Those self-righteous Pharisees should have seen themselves as the older brother in the story. Jesus' parable was for them, and the story was not supposed to end the way it did. It should have ended with a concerned older son seeing the distress of his grieving father and volunteering to go out in search of his lost brother. He should have followed the lost son to the far-off country, found him in the hog pen, assured him of his father's love, and brought him back. Could you picture the scene one afternoon if the anxious father, peering down the road, saw not one but two boys coming home, the older with his arm around the younger?

"Dad, I found him, and I've brought him home!"

It would be a completely happy ending. Every such story should end this way if we are the caring brother or sister that God wants us to be.

Lord, You have many lost sons and daughters.
I need Your grace to minister to the desperate
needs of those near me.

Journey to Phoenicia

Learn More

The Phoenicians were the maritime traders of the ancient world. Their ships sailed all over the Mediterranean, taking goods from one port to another. Their home ports included Tyre and Sidon, to the north of Palestine. The Phoenician alphabet, developed at Byblos, is considered to be the ancestor of our Roman alphabet.

Tyre was the most important of the Phoenician city-states. It was originally built on a rocky offshore island, which is now joined to the mainland. Tyre exists today as a seaport and the southernmost city of Lebanon. Less than 20 miles to the north is Sidon, another ancient seaport of the Phoenicians.

Read More

The story of Christ's healing of the Phoenician woman's daughter is told in Matthew 15:21-28 as well as in Mark 7:24-30. Jesus' reaction to this Gentile woman's petition was radically different from His usual kind and sympathetic approach to the sick and needy. Why was this the case?

39

Journey to Phoenicia

Jesus left and went to the region near the city of Tyre, where He stayed in someone's home. He did not want people to know He was there, but they found out anyway.

—Mark 7:24 (CEV)

ONLY TWICE DURING His earthly life did Jesus travel outside the boundaries of the Jewish state. The first trip was when He was a small child and was taken to Egypt by His parents to escape the death edict of King Herod, and the family remained there until Herod's death. Jesus' second trip abroad took place during His public ministry, when He travelled north from Galilee to the coastal cities of Phoenicia, accompanied by His disciples.

Jesus made this particular journey to avoid a threatening situation in Galilee, where Herod

Antipas had already imprisoned John the Baptist. The Jews did not regard Phoenicia as friendly territory, so Jesus intended to keep a low profile during His visit there. But his reputation as a healer had already spread beyond Israel. Suddenly, a Canaanite woman came running after him, crying out, "Lord, Son of David, have mercy on me! My daughter is cruelly afflicted with an evil spirit."

Jesus ignored her pleas. His disciples, believing their Master was reacting that way because the woman was a Gentile, said, "Let's send her away because she keeps crying out after us!" But the woman persisted and finally positioned herself right in front of Jesus. An interesting conversation followed.

"I am already busy dealing with the lost sheep of Israel," Jesus said to her.

She knelt at his feet. "Please help me."

Jesus shrugged. "It is not right to take bread out of children's mouths and throw it to dogs."

That response seemed okay to the disciples, but the woman saw a twinkle in His eyes that they did not see. "Yes, Lord," she said, "but even the dogs can eat the crumbs that fall from their master's table."

That was exactly what Christ wanted to hear. "Woman," He said, "you have great faith! Your request is granted. The evil spirit has already left your daughter."

Christ's disciples learned something important that day—something they would recall when He later gave them the commission to go into the whole world and preach the gospel to everyone. We must learn that same lesson in our encounters with people of all races and colors.

Lord, I thank You that Your love makes no distinctions of creed or color.

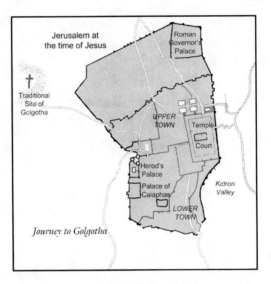

Jerusalem at
the time of Jesus

Roman
Governor's
Palace

Traditional
Site of
Golgotha

UPPER
TOWN

Temple

Court

Herod's
Palace

Palace of
Caiaphas

Kidron
Valley

LOWER
TOWN

Journey to Golgotha

Learn More

This approximate plan of ancient Jerusalem identifies sites
associated with the final 24 hours before Christ's crucifixion.
Some of the sites are known while others are conjectural,
based on the best information we have. On Thursday evening,
Jesus met with His disciples in an upper room in Jerusalem;
then they left the city, crossed the Kidron Valley, and entered
the Garden of Gethsemane. There, Jesus was arrested and
taken first to the high priest's palace and then to Pilate at the
Roman governor's palace. On Friday morning Jesus was taken
to Herod's palace, and then back to Pilate before the journey
to Golgotha, outside of the city.

Read More

All four Gospels preserve the account of Jesus' crucifixion and
death. John 19 is an especially compelling account that you
should read. Also read thoughtfully John 3:16-18. No one is
excluded from God's offer of salvation through Jesus.

40

Journey to Golgotha

Finally Pilate handed Him over to them to be crucified. So the soldiers took charge of Jesus. Carrying His own cross, He went out to the place of the Skull (which in Aramaic is called Golgotha).

—John 19:16-17 (NIV)

*P*ERHAPS THE JOURNEY to Golgotha began at the Incarnation, when the Son of God came to live among us, the cross set firmly before Him. However, we will focus here on the final agonizing steps of Friday morning, when Jesus was taken from Pilate's judgment hall to the hill of Golgotha just outside the walls of Jerusalem.

What thoughts troubled Jesus' mind as he trod that painful passage? Three years ago, He had personally selected 12 young men to be His special disciples. For three busy years He had trained and prepared them to take over where He knew He must leave off. They would now have the important task of taking His gospel to the world.

But were they ready for the task? As Jesus struggled down death row that morning, did His tortured mind recall that just 12 hours ago in the upper room, some of the Twelve were arguing as to who was the greatest among them? Did His mind replay the agonizing moments in the Garden of Gethsemane when His closest disciples preferred to sleep rather than pray with Him? What about the moment when Judas betrayed Him for a pocketful of silver? Did He hear again the cursing of Peter at last night's trial—the swear words of denial? Not one of those men was beside Him now, offering to carry the cross for Him.

In those darkest hours when He bore our sins and felt separation from His Father, could He know that those men would live and die for Him? Tradition tells us how that John would take the gospel to Ephesus, Peter to Rome, Thomas to India, Andrew to southern Greece, and Nathaniel and Thaddeus to Armenia. James would preach to the Jews, while Matthew would write a compelling account to bring the story of Christ to the whole world in ages to come. All except John would die a martyr's death, their blood, like seed, producing a rich harvest of souls.

And did the dying Jesus comprehend that 2,000 years into the future, millions would become His faithful disciples, bringing a message of peace, healing, and hope to a desperate world?

Thank You, dear Jesus. You endured the cross for me.

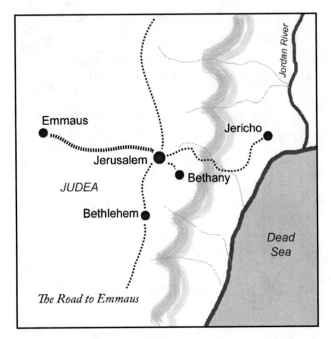

The Road to Emmaus

Learn More

There is uncertainty about the exact location of Emmaus. The name signifies "hot springs," and there is such a location approximately 20 miles west of Jerusalem. However, Luke, the Gospel writer, is considered to be a reliable source for geographical detail, and he gives the distance from Jerusalem to Emmaus as "about seven miles."

Read More

The story of the two disciples on the road to Emmaus told in Luke 24:13-35 is one to read and ponder. The two disciples did not recognize Jesus until they sat down and shared food with Him. By showing hospitality and kindness to someone in need, we are performing a Christ-like act. Also read Hebrews 13:2 and Matthew 25:31-40.

41

The Road to Emmaus

Now that same day two of them were going to a village called Emmaus, about seven miles from Jerusalem. They were talking with each other about everything that had happened.
—Luke 24:13-14 (NIV)

*T*WO MEN TRUDGED the seven weary miles from Jerusalem to Emmaus that Sunday afternoon. Despondent and discouraged, they could not erase the images of horror that played over and over in their minds. Less than 48 hours ago they had stood on a hillside outside Jerusalem, paralyzed by fear as they saw their beloved leader and master stripped, tortured, and crucified before their unbelieving eyes. It was a deathblow to their hopes that He was the Messiah, the military leader who would free Israel from the Roman yoke and establish a new kingdom. And if that was not bad enough, today the city of Jerusalem was astir with a story that someone had broken into Jesus' tomb and stolen the body. Some concluded that His disciples were responsible, so most of them were now hiding in an upper room, behind locked doors.

As the two men plodded home to Emmaus, recounting Friday's trauma in muted tones, a stranger caught up with them. He asked why they were troubled, so they shared the sad news. Although the stranger was seemingly unaware of the events in Jerusalem, He possessed a remarkable knowledge of the ancient Scriptures, which He shared with them as they walked. There was something compelling about the man and His words, but their bodies were too weary and their minds too preoccupied with the recent events to absorb everything He was saying.

The stranger was still sharing Scripture with them when they reached their village, so in the spirit of hospitality they invited Him for supper. It was just a simple meal, but when one of the men named Cleopas invited their guest to bless the food, something remarkable happened. Perhaps it was the way He raised His hands in blessing, or the words He spoke, but suddenly they knew that this stranger was the Master Himself! Jesus was alive!

With excitement and a new burst of energy, the two men headed back to Jerusalem. They had incredible news to share with the disciples. Their weariness gone, the two covered the seven miles in record time.

Two journeys. Same road and same two people. An encounter with Jesus made all the difference.

It still does.

Lord, when my journey is tiring and discouraging, please walk with me.

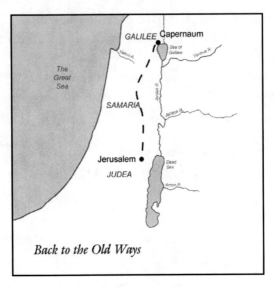

Back to the Old Ways

Learn More

It is likely that the seven discouraged disciples travelled to the lakeside near Capernaum, as that area had been their old home base for fishing before Jesus called them. The seven in this story were Peter, Thomas, Nathaniel, James, John, and two other disciples not named (see John 21:1-2).

Read More

Read John 21:1-16. The events of this story happened some days after Jesus' death and resurrection. Following His resurrection, Jesus appeared briefly to some of His disciples on at least two occasions. While this should have encouraged them, they were undoubtedly feeling heavily the loss of their Master. He had been such a consistent part of their lives for three busy years. Tumultuous change can affect our lives as painfully as it did for those seven disciples. At those times, we must remember that Jesus has not abandoned us, just as He had not abandoned His followers then.

4 2

Back to the Old Ways

Simon Peter said, "I'm going fishing!" The others said, "We will go with you." They went out in their boat. But they didn't catch a thing that night.
—John 21:3 (CEV)

*A*S THE SUN sets over Lake Galilee, seven men climb into their old fishing boat and pole out into deeper water. Darkness falls as they cast the net for a night of fishing. They work in silence, the blackness of the night matching the gloom of their thoughts. It has been more than three years since they last worked their nets together.

Only three years? It seems like an eternity. Their minds revert to an unforgettable day when a compelling young teacher walked down to the lakeshore and invited them to become His specially chosen disciples. "Follow me," He had said. And they had responded, abandoning their traditional ways for a new life of incredible magnitude. Three amazing years! But then, just days ago, their Master had been seized, beaten, and publicly crucified. The memories are still fresh and painful.

At the first light of dawn, the seven tired men haul in the empty net and slowly pole back toward the shore. Their night of fishing has been a failure. It is not like it used to be. They feel defeated, their souls empty and gasping like a fish out of the water.

"Did you catch anything?"

All heads turn toward the beach. In the half-light they have not noticed the dark form of a man standing at the water's edge.

"No." There is nothing more to say.

"Cast your net again, on the other side of the boat."

Then everything happens quickly. Seven excited men are hauling a net so full of fish that it takes every ounce of their strength to pull it in. Minutes later they are hugging Jesus, their Master, with even more excitement. He gathers them around a fire to warm their shivering bodies, supplies a hot breakfast to fill their empty stomachs, and then, as the sunshine of a new day bursts upon the lakeshore, He gives them a purpose for living. His words, though addressed to Peter, are for all of them. "Feed my sheep," He says. "Your fishing days are over. Now you will be my shepherds." The seven become evangelists, never to return to fishing.

Once you've had a personal relationship with Jesus, there is no turning back. Fishing is not the same as it used to be.

Thank You, Lord, for the joy of Your presence. I can't go back to the old ways.

On the Desert Road to Gaza

Learn More

In New Testament times, there was a flourishing Jewish community in Ethiopia. The origin of this community may date from the time the Israelites lived in Egypt, as the Nile was a trade route into the interior of northern Africa. Centuries later, the Queen of Sheba (a broad region that included Ethiopia) visited King Solomon (see 1 Kings 10:1-13).

Gaza was one of five federated cities of the Philistines. At the time of the Israelite conquest, the territory of Gaza was mentioned as one of three cities that Joshua was not able to subdue (see Josh. 11:21-22). Later, Samson visited Gaza and was almost captured by the Philistines (see Judg. 16:1-2).

Read More

Read the story of the Ethiopian's journey in Acts 8:26-40. God sometimes brings us into contact with someone who is desperate to hear the good news. God still calls individuals to Africa to go as ambassadors for His kingdom and provide humanitarian assistance to the poor and needy.

43

On the Desert Road to Gaza

You shall be witnesses to Me in Jerusalem, and in all Judea and Samaria, and to the ends of the earth.
—Acts 1:8 (NKJV)

*J*UST BEFORE HIS ascension, Jesus predicted that the good news of salvation would penetrate the remote corners of the earth. The New Testament book of Acts tells how that drama began to unfold.

Act One. Philip the Evangelist, one of seven deacons chosen by the apostles, is in Samaria, baptizing many into the fledgling Christian community. Then, right in the midst of his evangelistic program, Philip is instructed by the Lord to abandon his preaching and travel south to the desert road connecting Jerusalem with the seaport of Gaza. It does not make sense, but Philip obeys his Lord.

Act Two. A black African Jew has made the long pilgrimage from Ethiopia to Jerusalem to attend the rites of Passover, an annual event in the Jewish calendar. This man is no ordinary individual but the treasurer of the Ethiopian nation, serving at the court of Queen Candace. No visitor to Jerusalem at this Passover time can escape the fact that this is also the anniversary of Jesus' crucifixion. The growing Christian community is experiencing intense persecution, yet the message of a risen Christ is proclaimed everywhere. The visitor from Ethiopia is puzzled by it all, but it leads him back to the Scriptures that foretell the coming of the Messiah.

Act Three. The African official is on his way home, travelling by the desert road to Gaza, where he will board a ship to Egypt and then journey up the Nile to Ethiopia. As he is seated in his chariot, he reads aloud from the scrolls of the prophet Isaiah, his mind bursting with questions. Suddenly, he is joined by a man who is able to explain the fulfilment of the messianic prophecies. It is Philip, and before the day's journey is over, the Ethiopian has converted to Christianity. They stop the carriage by a pool of water where Philip baptizes him.

In this way, an unnamed Ethiopian became the first Christian foreign missionary, taking the good news of Jesus Christ to the continent of Africa. By the time the apostle Paul was setting out on his first missionary journey, the Christian flag was already flying in "the ends of the earth."

The good news now encircles the world, yet there are still unreached groups of people who have not heard the gospel. We must pray daily for those who take the story of Jesus to remote corners of earth.

Lord, please help me to be a "missionary,"
whether that is in Africa or in my own
community.

Mission to Caesarea

Learn More

Caesarea (literally, the "city of Caesar") was built by Herod the Great in honor of the Roman emperor. It was located 23 miles south of Mount Carmel. Caesarea became the capital of the Roman province of Palestine and Syria.

Joppa was an ancient seaport of the Phoenicians and the place where Jonah went to find a ship sailing to Tarshish (see Jon. 1:3). The city became the primary port for Jerusalem (it was located 35 miles away) when King Solomon had cedars from Lebanon brought there on floats. Today, modern Joppa (Jaffa) adjoins the city of Tel Aviv.

Read More

Read the amazing account in Acts 10:1-48 of how God brought a Jew and a Gentile together by giving each a vision. In contrast to the apostle Peter's deeply ingrained attitude toward the Gentiles, we find a Roman centurion who gave generously to the poor in his community and was respected by the Jewish people. Can we today learn something from the gracious acts of many non-Christians?

44

Mission to Caesarea

Peter began to speak: "I now realize how true it is that God does not show favoritism but accepts men from every nation who fear him and do what is right."

—Acts 10:34-35 (NIV)

EVER SINCE PENTECOST, when the Holy Spirit came upon the disciples with conviction and power, they had been fulfilling their commission to preach the gospel. Their focus, though, was exclusively for the Jews. Gentiles were "unclean" and considered outside the pale of salvation. But the time had come for that to change.

God sent Peter to the port of Joppa, where he stayed at the seaside home of Simon the Tanner. One day about noon, Peter climbed steps to the rooftop overlooking the blue Mediterranean, where he followed his custom of mid-day meditation. During his time of prayer, God gave him a strange vision. Peter saw a large sheet filled with all kinds of wild animals and reptiles appear before him, and then a voice commanded, "Get up, Peter. Kill and eat."

The apostle was shocked. "Surely not, Lord," he said. "I've never eaten anything impure or unclean." Strict adherence to Jewish dietary laws had always been part of his lifestyle. But the voice responded, "Do not call anything impure that God has made clean." Then the sheet disappeared.

As Peter was pondering the meaning of the vision, three men were knocking at the gate below, asking for him. They introduced themselves as servants of a Roman centurion named Cornelius who lived at Caesarea, an important coastal city to the north. "Our master had a vision from God, who told him to send for you, sir," they said.

Puzzled, Peter asked how they knew to find him there in Joppa.

"Our master was given instructions that we would find you here at the house of Simon the Tanner," they answered.

Uncertain, but sensing that God was summoning him, Peter accompanied the men back to Caesarea, where he met Cornelius. There, he discovered that the centurion had invited a large group of people to his house to hear whatever Peter had to say. Peter preached the gospel of Jesus Christ to that large gathering of Gentiles that day, and he remained with them several days, conducting a baptism and organizing the first Christian congregation outside the Jewish community.

Are we sometimes guilty of excluding people who belong to a different culture or ethnic group?

I'm thankful, Lord, that You offer salvation freely to everyone.

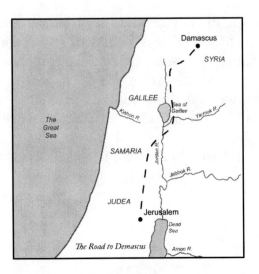

The Road to Damascus

Learn More

It is claimed that Damascus is the oldest continuously inhabited city in the world. It has been the capital of Syria since ancient times. Paul's vision occurred on the road from Jerusalem as he and his party approached Damascus.

Read More

Read Luke's account of the Damascus Road event in Acts 9:1-19. Then read Paul's own description of the experience, as he later told it to King Agrippa, in Acts 26:9-18. We can imagine the total disbelief of both Christians and Jews when they were told that Saul, the Christian-beater, had made a complete turnaround and was now preaching Jesus Christ. Read about the reactions of Ananias in Acts 9:13-14, the believers in Damascus in Acts 9:19-22, the Jewish leaders in Acts 9:23-25, and Jesus' own disciples in Acts 9:26. The single exception was Barnabas, a Christian gentleman who befriended Paul and salvaged the situation (see Acts 9:27-28). New believers in our day need individuals like Barnabas to welcome them into the fellowship of faith.

45

The Road to Damascus

On one of these journeys I was going to Damascus
with the authority and commission of the chief
priests. About noon...as I was on the road, I saw a
light from heaven, brighter than the sun, blazing
around me and my companions.

—Acts 26:12-13 (NIV)

*A*N EXECUTION WAS taking place outside of
Jerusalem. Death by stoning. The victim was
Stephen, a courageous Christian who was accused of
blasphemy. The stone-throwers were Jewish officials,
members of the High Priest's council. Standing
nearby was a young fellow named Saul. He minded
their robes while they hurled rocks, and applauded
their action.

Saul had a bright future in the Jewish hierarchy.
Educated in the school of one of Judaism's most

respected scholars and teachers, Saul was committed to defending the Jewish faith and exterminating Christians. He was a ruthless henchman, going about with his band of soldiers in his relentless pursuit of those who took the name of Jesus. Once he found them, he would have them thrown into prison, where they would be tortured or stoned to death for their faith.

Christians feared Saul because of his extreme hatred of them and his zeal in persecuting those he captured. But try as he might, Saul was unsuccessful in rooting out the heresy. Just when he thought he had the situation under control in one place, there would be outbreaks of Christian belief in a dozen new places.

Hearing reports of Christian communities in Damascus, Saul and his entourage set out for the Syrian capital. The group was almost within sight of the city when it happened. A blinding flash, hot as a lightning bolt, threw the men to the ground. Then a voice like thunder said, "Saul, what do you think you are doing? Do you really believe you can stop the spread of My Kingdom?" In that instant, Saul found himself face to face with the resurrected Jesus.

"Listen to me, Saul!" the Lord said. "I have a commission for you. I want you to be my ambassador to the Gentiles and preach my gospel to the entire world." Exit Saul the relentless persecutor of Christ's followers. Enter Paul the intrepid apostle of Jesus.

Some journeys are life-changing experiences. Something happens along the way that turns our life around, and things are never the same again.

Dear Jesus, I acknowledge You as my Savior and Lord of my life.

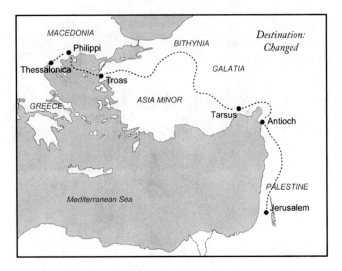

Learn More

Troas was located a short distance southwest of ancient Troy. Excavations have uncovered remains of city walls, a temple, a theater, and a gymnasium, all dating from the time of Paul.

The Macedonians were an ancient people who inhabited the northern part of the Greek peninsula. Alexander the Great came from Macedonia. The ruins of ancient Philippi are inland, about five miles from the port city of Kavala, which was called Neapolis in Paul's day. Remains of the old Roman road, the Egnation Way leading from Neapolis to Philippi, are still visible today.

Read More

Read the story of how God blocked Paul's travel plans in Acts 16:6-15. Luke the physician wrote the book of Acts, and he accompanied and supported Paul on his missionary travels in Macedonia. Foreign missionary ventures still depend on helpers of many kinds—doctors, nurses, teachers, engineers, cooks, builders, and pilots, to name just a few.

4 6

Destination: Changed

*Paul and his friends went through Phrygia and
Galatia, but the Holy Spirit would not let them
preach in Asia. After they arrived in Mysia, they
tried to go into Bithynia, but the Spirit of Jesus
would not let them.*

—Acts 16:6-7 (CEV)

*I*F YOU HAVE ever had your travel plans messed
up because of political interference, cancelled
flights, or anything else outside of your control, you
will understand the frustrations Paul had during his
second evangelistic itinerary.

Paul's plans for this missionary tour seemed to
be falling apart. On a previous trip, the apostle had
carved out a Christian presence in several towns
and cities in southeastern Asia Minor. Now this

ambitious man had his sights set on the rest of Asia Minor. He intended to push the boundaries of God's kingdom northward to the Black Sea.

But his plans were not working out. Whenever he tried to enter a new territory, the Lord threw up roadblocks. Prevented from going north or east, Paul wondered if his trip would end in failure and retreat. Frustrated and perplexed, he turned in the only direction left to him and trekked westward.

Arriving at the port city of Troas, Paul may have assumed that he had come to the end of his territory. As he gazed out upon the waters of the Aegean Sea, sparkling in the western sun, he knew that the lands of Macedonia and Greece lay somewhere across that sea. Further to the west was Italy, the heartland of the Roman Empire, and beyond that was the vast region of Europe. All this territory was yet untouched by the gospel. Countless unreached peoples.

God had an exciting project in mind for Paul. In a dream, Paul saw a man beckoning to him from across the sea, pleading, "Please come over into Macedonia and help us!" Paul accepted the challenge. He and his companions found a ship crossing from Troas to Macedonia, where the Roman city of Philippi was his first stopping place.

So Paul answered the call of God, turning his attention to the continent of Europe. His willingness to follow God's leading would forever change the history of Europe and Christianity.

Never underestimate God's purpose for your life. It may be bigger than you have imagined!

There are times, Lord, when I don't know which way to turn. I pray for direction in my life.

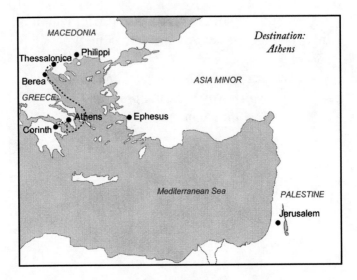

Learn More

After crossing into Macedonia from Troas in Asia Minor, Paul raised up churches in Philippi, Thessalonica, and Berea. It was from Berea that Paul sailed to Athens. Visitors to modern Athens can explore the area of the old marketplace (Agora) on the northern side of the Acropolis and climb to the rocky summit of Mars Hill (Areopagus) where the ancient councils of the city and the high court met.

Read More

Read about Paul's traumatic experiences in Philippi in Acts 16:16-40, in Thessalonica in Acts 17:1-9, and in Berea in Acts 17:10-15. Most of us would have given up and gone home long before this. What do you think inspired Paul to continue with his mission? Like Paul, there are men and women in our day who endure suffering and life threats in faraway countries while pursuing the cause of Christ. We must pray for them.

Destination: Athens

All the Athenians and the foreigners who lived there
spent their time doing nothing but talking about and
listening to the latest ideas. Paul then stood up in
the meeting of the Areopagus.

—Acts 17:21-22 (NIV)

*P*AUL HAD NOT planned to be in Athens at
that time. He and his team had been busy
establishing churches throughout the northern
province of Macedonia. But troublemakers were
threatening Paul's life, and his companions, fearing
for his safety, had urged him to leave the area.
Friends escorted him by ship to Athens, where he
was to await the arrival of Silas and Timothy, his
co-workers.

But Paul was not very good at waiting. Seized with the unexpected opportunity to witness for Christ in the world's center of culture, religion, and learning, Paul went to the Jewish synagogue on the Sabbath and to the marketplace during the week. Never failing to attract a crowd, Paul soon had a group of philosophers arguing with him.

"What are you babbling about?" they sneered. "Come with us to the Areopagus and let the city fathers decide what to do with you!" They led Paul up to the Acropolis, where the magnificent Parthenon temple held pride of place, overlooking the city. A rocky eminence nearby was the meeting place of the city's governors. Placing Paul in front of a group of learned Athenians, they asked, "What is this strange new teaching that you have?"

Paul met the challenge. Using his fine educational background and oratorical skills, he launched into a scholarly exposition of Scripture, even quoting from Greek philosophers. It was a fine sermon, but it brought no conviction in the minds of the hearers. When Paul journeyed on to Corinth soon afterward, he left behind barely a handful of people who were interested in the gospel message. It is significant that we have Paul's letters to churches he established in Philippi, Thessalonica, Ephesus, and other places, but no letter to a church in Athens.

Writing much later to the congregation at Corinth, Paul reminisced, "When I came to you, brothers, I did not come with eloquence or superior wisdom as I proclaimed to you the testimony about God" (1 Cor. 2:1, NIV). We are sometimes guilty of entangling the simple message of Jesus with complex discussion and theological jargon.

Lord, there are many desperate people who don't know that Jesus loves them and died for them. Please give me the courage to tell them.

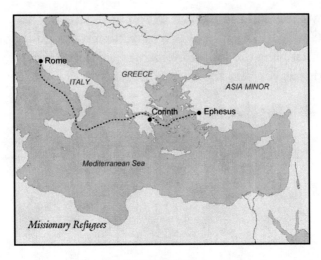

Missionary Refugees

Learn More

The important city of Corinth was situated on a narrow strip of land that joined the Peloponnesus with mainland Greece, so Corinth had access by sea to Ephesus in the east and Rome in the west. Modern-day visitors to the ruins of Corinth can walk through the ancient marketplace where the tentmakers probably carried on their business.

Ephesus was the major commercial and trading port of western Asia. It was also the location of the magnificent Temple of Artemis, one of the seven wonders of the ancient world. This temple was destroyed in 356 B.C. and replaced by a new but less extravagant temple, which stood there in Paul's day.

Read More

Read about Paul's ministry in Corinth in Acts 18. During a later visit to the city, Paul wrote his letter to the Christians in Rome. By that time Aquila and Priscilla were back in Rome. You can read Paul's greeting to them in Romans 16:3 and their shared greetings to the church at Corinth sent from Ephesus in 1 Corinthians 16:19.

48

Missionary Refugees

*Give my greetings to Priscilla and Aquila, my
fellow-workers in Christ Jesus. They risked their
necks to save my life, and not I alone but all the
gentile congregations are grateful to them.*
—Romans 16:3-4 (NEB)

*A*QUILA AND PRISCILLA were a Jewish
couple living in Rome. During those times
every Jewish boy learned a trade, so Aquila learned
the craft of making tents, which were in constant
demand for military purposes. Aquila taught the
trade to his wife, Priscilla, so the two operated a
business partnership.

When trouble erupted within the Jewish
community in Rome, Emperor Claudius banished
all Jews from the city, forcing Aquila and his wife
to flee to Corinth in southern Greece, where they

again set up their tentmaking business. Some time later, Paul arrived in Corinth. As a young man, he had also been taught the craft of tentmaking, so on meeting the Jewish refugee couple from Rome, he joined their business part-time while he worked to raise up a Christian congregation in the city. Aquila and Priscilla accepted the new faith and became members of the Christian church at Corinth.

When Paul sailed for Ephesus some time later, Aquila and Priscilla accompanied him, eager to assist the missionary apostle in bringing the gospel message to another important city of the Roman Empire. After a short time in Ephesus, with a promise to return soon, the apostle headed back to Jerusalem, leaving Aquila and Priscilla to carry on the work he had started.

In their quiet but effective way, the tentmakers soon had a small congregation meeting in their home. Later, another convert, Apollos, arrived from Alexandria. Apollos was a preacher, but he lacked an understanding of some points of doctrine. So Aquila and his wife invited the newcomer to come to their home and quietly shared their broader understanding of the gospel message. To his credit, Apollos listened and became an even more effective evangelist.

Years later when Paul wrote his letter to the church at Rome, Aquila and Priscilla were back in their home city, their house again a meeting place for Christians. They were just a dedicated couple of tentmakers, but their Christian influence was strong and far-reaching. "They risked their necks for me," Paul wrote, "and not only I, but all the churches of the Gentiles, are grateful to them."

There are places in the Islamic world where preachers are not welcome, but there is always an opportunity for "tentmakers."

Whatever my vocation, Lord, help me witness to Your love and grace.

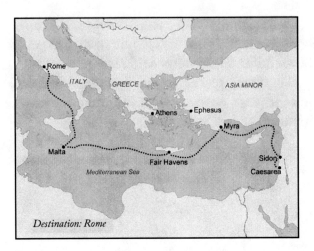

Destination: Rome

Learn More

On the island of Malta is a walled town now known as Mdina that is located on the summit of a prominent hill. The Phoenicians originally fortified this town around 700 B.C., naming it Melita. When the island later came under Roman rule, a governor's palace was built on the hilltop, and it was probably here that Paul was entertained by Governor Publius. Within the walls today are several palaces being restored, but the most prominent edifice is St. Paul's Cathedral, built on the site of an early Christian church.

Read More

Acts 27, the gripping story of a raging storm ending with a shipwreck, is one of the most descriptive narratives in Scripture. It is a first-person account written by Luke, a physician who accompanied Paul on his voyage as a prisoner to Rome and remained with him there (see Col. 4:14; 2 Tim. 4:11; Philem. 24). Providing companionship and support to someone in need is a special kind of practical Christianity. In fact, in Paul's list of spiritual gifts, he included "those able to help others" (see 1 Cor. 12:28).

Destination: Rome

When daylight came, they did not recognize the land, but they saw a bay with a sandy beach, where they decided to run the ship aground if they could....Once safely on shore, we found that the island was Malta.

—Acts 27:39; 28:1 (NIV)

*T*HE VOYAGE BEGAN at a port in Palestine, where several prisoners were herded onto a ship with a guard of Roman soldiers. Paul, the missionary apostle, was one of them. Conditions on board were miserable, but Paul was fortunate to have his physician friend, Luke, accompanying him on the voyage. During a short stop in Asia Minor, the prisoners were transferred to another ship bound for Rome. Altogether, there were 276 persons on board, a motley company of prisoners, soldiers, paying passengers, and crew.

Winter was approaching, the season of storms in the Mediterranean. Despite receiving a warning message, the captain set sail westward toward Italy. Soon, however, the weather turned ugly, as hurricane-force winds battered the vessel. Desperate to save the ship, the crew threw cargo overboard, but as the storm raged on, the exhausted men gave up all hope of survival.

But Paul had a message of hope for everyone. An angel had appeared to him in the night with the assurance that he would arrive in Rome to be tried before Caesar. "Keep up your courage, men," he said, "for I have faith in God that it will happen just as he told me. Nevertheless, we will run aground on some island."

The island turned out to be Malta. The vessel was blown onto a sandbar, where the stern was smashed to pieces by the pounding waves. It was raining and miserably cold as everyone struggled ashore, but the islanders proved friendly and built a large fire to warm the shivering survivors. Paul now had everyone's respect. Soon he and Luke were escorted to the hilltop city of Melita to be personally entertained by the governor, Publius. For most of the survivors, the shipwreck meant a winter of waiting on Malta for the onward journey to Rome, but for Paul it meant an unexpected opportunity to grow a Christian community in yet another corner of the world.

When our lives are shattered by circumstances beyond our control, we can have confidence that God has not abandoned us.

Wherever my journeys take me, Lord, please come with me.

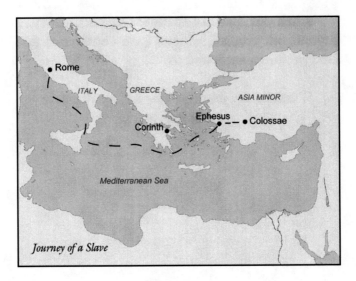

Journey of a Slave

Learn More

Slavery was part of the culture of ancient times and was extremely important to the Roman economy. Only the poor were unable to afford slaves. During every conquest, the Romans captured people and sold them into slavery. The small island of Delos in the Aegean Sea was a wholesale slave market where up to 10,000 slaves were sold on a daily basis. Slaves worked in mines and as agricultural laborers, house servants, child nannies and in the Coliseum as gladiators.

Located on an ancient trade route, Colossae was an important city during Roman times. Paul's letter to the church at Colossae (Colossians) was written while he was a prisoner in Rome and was probably carried, along with his private letter to Philemon, in the care of Tychicus and Onesimus (see Col. 4:7-9).

Read More

Paul's letter to Philemon is one of the shortest books of the Bible. Most of the letter is a touching appeal to Philemon on behalf of his runaway slave.

Journey of a Slave

*I appeal to you for my son, Onesimus, who became
my son while I was in chains....Welcome him as you
would welcome me. If he has done you any wrong
or owes you anything, charge it to me.*
—Philemon 10,17-18 (NIV)

THE STORY BEGINS at Colossae in Asia Minor.
Onesimus is a slave in the service of Philemon,
a man of wealth who is also a Christian. One day,
Onesimus, obsessed with the urge to be free, robs
his master and bolts. He makes his way to Rome,
where he tries to lose himself in the milling crowds
of the great city. But he carries the mark of a slave
on his body, so he cannot escape the nagging fear
that he will be recognized, arrested, and returned to
Colossae for severe punishment.

Rome is a cold city without a heart, and in his fear and loneliness Onesimus is drawn to the warmth and acceptance of the small Christian community. He is soon introduced to Paul the apostle, who is now confined within the dark Mamertine Prison, his hands chained to the damp rock wall of the cell. Paul's public voice has been silenced, but with a support network of faithful friends, he is busy dictating letters to the churches he established throughout the Roman world. Onesimus becomes one of Paul's volunteer helpers, and their relationship develops into that of a father and son.

"Onesimus, my son," Paul says one day, "I have written to my dear friend Philemon, who is also your master. I need someone to go to Colossae and deliver my letter to him."

The young man's stomach churns at the thought. He knows that he can expect a flogging and a branding on his forehead as a fugitive when he returns. But he is now a servant of Jesus, and he knows that he must return to his master and beg forgiveness. It is a tough decision, but he decides to go and take Paul's letter with him. The letter assures Philemon that Onesimus has now accepted the Lord Jesus as his master and that he should be welcomed home as a brother.

The story is a beautiful illustration of the transformation that occurs in the heart of one who accepts the saving grace of Jesus. More than that, it is the incredible wonder of a God who not only forgives returning runaways but also treats them as His own sons and daughters.

Thank You, Lord, for Your forgiveness and grace.

Amazing Love!

And can it be that I should gain
an interest in the Savior's blood?
Died He for me, who caused His pain?
For me?—who Him to death pursued?
Amazing love! How can it be
that Thou, my God, shouldst die for me?

He left His Father's throne above
(so free, so infinite His grace!),
emptied Himself of all but love,
and bled for Adam's helpless race.
'Tis mercy all, immense and free,
for O my God, it found out me!

Long my imprisoned spirit lay,
fast bound in sin and nature's night;
Thine eye diffused a quickening ray;
I woke, the dungeon flamed with light;
my chains fell off, my heart was free,
I rose, went forth, and followed Thee.

No condemnation now I dread;
Jesus and all in Him, is mine.
Alive in Him, my living Head,
and clothed in righteousness divine,
bold I approach the eternal throne,
and claim the crown, through Christ my own!

—Charles Wesley, 1739

51

The Ultimate Journey

The Word became a human being and lived here with us. We saw His true glory, the glory of the only Son of the Father.

—John 1:14 (CEV)

*T*HROUGH THE AGES, there have been many great and amazing journeys taken by humankind: Marco Polo's overland trek from Europe to China; the voyage of Christopher Columbus to the New World; H.M. Stanley's journey into the heart of Africa to find Livingstone; Lindbergh's pioneering solo flight across the Atlantic from New York to Paris; man's first space voyage to the moon.

These journeys were great, even incredible, but the greatest journey ever taken happened about 2,000 years ago when the Son of God came all the way from heaven to earth to become the Son of Man. It was a journey of immeasurable and unimaginable distance, across the span of the universe, through trillions of light years, to one small planet of our solar system. What a journey!

But to contemplate this greatest of all journeys is not to think about distance. True, its length is mind-boggling, but what is incomprehensible is its depth. Paul the apostle describes it this way: "Christ Jesus, who, being in very nature God... made himself nothing...and being found in appearance as a man, he humbled himself and became obedient to death—even death on a cross!" (Phil. 2:5-8). The Creator became the creature and died a cruel and shameful death. It is beyond our understanding.

Yet it is also the most glorious event this planet has ever experienced. The greatest journey undertaken by God makes possible the greatest journey that any human being can ever take—a single, faltering step toward Jesus Christ and salvation! It is a simple step of faith and belief. Millions have taken that step and have experienced forgiveness, acceptance, joy, and new life. Sadly, millions more have declined to take that one small step, turning their backs on Jesus and eternal life.

Thank You, Lord, for the incomprehensible journey of love You took for me. I accept Your free, gracious gift of salvation today.

CHRIST'S JOURNEY HOME AS TOLD BY LUKE

During the forty days after His crucifixion
He appeared to the apostles from time to
time, actually alive,
and proved to them in many ways
that it was really He Himself they were seeing.
And on those occasions He talked to them
about the Kingdom of God.

In one of these meetings He told them not to
leave Jerusalem
until the Holy Spirit came upon them
in fulfillment of the Father's promise,
a matter He had previously
discussed with them.

It was not long afterwards that He rose into the sky
and disappeared into a cloud, leaving them
staring after Him.
As they were straining their eyes for
another glimpse,
suddenly two white-robed men were standing
there among them, and said,
"Men of Galilee, why are you standing here
staring at the sky?
Jesus has gone away to Heaven,
and some day, just as He went,
He will return!"

—Acts 1:3-4, 9-11 (TLB)

The Journey Home

*Let not your heart be troubled. You are trusting God,
now trust in me. There are many homes up there
where my Father lives, and I am going to prepare
them for your coming. When everything is ready,
then I will come and get you, so that you can always
be with me where I am.*

—John 14:1-3 (TLB)

$\mathcal{I}$T WAS THURSDAY night, the night before
the trial and crucifixion. Jesus and the Twelve
had assembled in an upper room in Jerusalem to
celebrate Passover, the last meal they would have
together. The disciples would never forget those
moments. Dismay and anguish filled their hearts as
their Master revealed the imminence of His death.
Shock numbed their minds at the discovery that

Judas Iscariot, one of their own, had betrayed their beloved Master. Their hearts were indeed troubled.

Looking around at their anxious faces, Jesus shared something amazing with them. Yes, He would leave them and return to His Father, but He would also be preparing homes for them in heaven. When everything was ready, He would come back and take them home to live with Him forever.

For those troubled disciples, Jesus' promise was full of meaning. They knew about wedding customs in their society. They knew that a prospective bridegroom, after the engagement or betrothal, would return to his parents' home and there prepare a home for his bride. When the house was ready, the bridegroom would come back for his bride and escort her to their new home. A joyful wedding celebration would follow. In the same way, the disciples' beloved Master, their Bridegroom, was going away to prepare a home for them. He would return one day to take them home with Him for a great celestial wedding celebration! They would be with Him forever!

Jesus' promise is for us, too. Life on planet earth is but a journey. We are pilgrims here. We may enjoy the scenery and the friendships along the way, but deep down we all have hearts longing for home—a place where we will belong forever. That is why Jesus' promise to the disciples is also especially for us. "I will come again," He says, "and take you home."

Thank You, my Lord Jesus, for that amazing promise. By God's grace I will be with You there.

Other Books by Keith Clouten

Hunter Valley Bushwalk
Playing Our Past
Reid's Mistake

Keith lives at Lacombe, Alberta,
Canada and can be contacted
by e-mail at: Clouten1@telus.net